M000043037

A Cat's Guide to Humans

Also by Celia Haddon

One Hundred Ways to Say I Love You

One Hundred Secret Thoughts
Cats Have About Humans

One Hundred Ways for a Cat
to Find Its Inner Kitten

One Hundred Ways for a Cat to Train its Human

100 Ways to Be More Like Your Cat

100 Ways to Be As Happy As Your Dog

A Cat's Guide to Humans

From A to Z

George the Cat
Owner of Celia Haddon

First published in Great Britain in 2019 by Yellow Kite
An imprint of Hodder & Stoughton
An Hachette UK company

2

Illustrations © Jilly Wilkinson

A CIP catalogue record for this title is available from the British Library

Hardback ISBN 978 1 529 35300 6
eBook ISBN 978 1 529 35301 3

Typeset in Celeste by Hewer Text UK Ltd, Edinburgh
Printed and bound in Great Britain by Clays Ltd, Elcograf S.p.A.

Hodder & Stoughton policy is to use papers that are natural, renewable and recyclable products and made from wood grown in sustainable forests. The logging and manufacturing processes are expected to conform to the environmental regulations of the country of origin.

Yellow Kite
Hodder & Stoughton Ltd
Carmelite House
50 Victoria Embankment
London EC4Y 0DZ

www.yellowkitebooks.co.uk

To Professor Daniel Mills who taught Celia about cats. He is not responsible for my feline opinions.

Introduction

So you want a human of your very own. The rewards are obvious – a warm house, regular meals, and (if you care for it) petting, the human idea of grooming. Adopting a pet human is a responsibility. Humans need quite a high level of feline care, if the relationship is to be successful. You will have to work at making it happen. This book is designed to help you care for and understand your human.

Is understanding your human necessary? Some cats take the view that if the meals are served on time, the heating is correctly adjusted and the beds soft, then it is not necessary to forge an intimate relationship with this species. They will eat their breakfasts and disappear through the cat flap, only returning for meals and sleep. However, treating the house as if it is a hotel and ignoring your human altogether is morally wrong. The poor creatures depend on us for affection and nurturing. Part of taking on a human pet is to pay proper attention to its emotional needs, as well as your own physical requirements.

All conscientious owners would like to be able to communicate better with their human pets. Some cats argue that humans are unable to think or feel, that they are simply large naked automatons. Most of us dispute this. Careful observation shows that humans are more intelligent than we previously thought. They are capable of 'thinking', though they think differently from us. They have good memories and they can learn from experience. Their behaviour also shows that they have similar emotions of desire, fear, anger, panic, play, care and lust – though they express these in ways that may seem strange to us.

Time spent on the lap is never wasted. In the long run, increasing a human's affection for you will result in better human service. They need to feel loved and making them feel loved does not take too much time and effort. Be willing to pay them attention and you will find that you reap dividends in the way of cat treats. Firmness and kindness are the principles of human management.

As a behaviourist, I have spent my life studying humans. I took an honours degree in applied human behaviour to help understand them. A subsequent master's degree in clinical human behaviour enabled me to advise other cats about common human problems. These include the problems of human sexuality as it impacts on cats, partner change and the difficulties that this can cause us, and irritating habits such as selfies and staring.

This book will help you learn what humans are trying to express and give you a better chance of guessing what they are 'thinking'. Many of the problems that occur between cats and humans can be prevented, managed or even cured, if we understand them better. I have therefore highlighted some of the ways in which we can train, manage and enjoy this different species. I also give useful tips about the practical aspects of living with a single human or surviving in a multi-human household.

The welfare of our humans is in our own paws.

A is for . . .

Adopting a Human – Off the Street

If you are living on the street or looking for a new home, do a thorough home check before you move in. Has the human been trained by its previous feline owner? Does it offer the right brand of cat food? Does its home have good access to hunting fields? Does the human know its place: i.e., is it aware that you require household services of a high quality? If everything seems suitable for you, move in fast before some other cat gets there before you.

Just walk in if doors or windows are open, and go up to the nearest human with an inquiring look on your face. Meow interrogatively. If you are in a kitchen, look for a crumb of dry bread on the floor and eat it ravenously. You may not be at all hungry, but it is important to *appear* starving. Food is the way to a human's heart. Most of them love feeding cats and the first stage in your relationship is to encourage them to do so by looking hungry. If you are already being fed, then you will have to fake it.

If there isn't any food around, then you will have to rely on a display of unrestrained affection. Walk over to them and rub their legs, purring loudly. Jump on their laps, if these are available, and settle down immediately. You don't actually have to be a lap cat: you only have to *appear* to be one temporarily. Don't be afraid to fake affection. Most humans are flattered if a cat shows it wants their company. Poor souls, they often don't really know what we have in mind. These initial encounters are so deeply pleasing to them, that they become putty in our paws. Before they fully realise what they are doing, they have become a pet human, or as they see it a cat 'owner'.

Adoption from a Cat Shelter

If you are banged up in a rescue shelter and you cannot do a home check, you have to rely on your ability to assess a suitable human pet from their behaviour. Quiet and calm humans are the best bet. When you see a human you like, move to the front of the rehoming pen, and purr loudly. Rub your face against the bars. Try an imploring meow. If you don't like the look of them, give them a lingering look of contempt, turn your back on them and hide in the bed area.

Adoption – Choosing Your Human

- **OLDIES.** These have usually had staff experience in looking after cats. Now that age has 'neutered' them, they are likely to be in a quiet household with nothing much to do except care for you. They stay at home all day with the heating on, instead of leaving home for eight to ten hours a day at work. Their routine is not dissimilar to ours – get up, eat food, nap, eat food, nap, eat food, nap with TV, eat food, night-time sleep.

- **SINGLETONS.** Always better than couples or families. They have more time to devote to you and usually become emotionally dependent upon you very quickly indeed. However online dating may lead to unacceptable night time activity. They may start bringing home mates for hot sessions at night on your bed. It's difficult to get a good night's sleep when there is too much going on underneath the duvet.

- **YOUNG MALE/FEMALE COUPLES.** If you are energetic and confident, these can be fun. However, there is the danger of pregnancy, babies and toddlers. These take the focus off proper cat care.

- **SAME SEX COUPLES.** These make great pets. Slightly less chance of the patter of tiny human feet and thus more time to devote to cats.

- **BUSY WORKING HUMANS.** These will suit your lifestyle if you are too busy to have much time for humans. They will function as bed and breakfast providers, and the rest of the day you are left to get on with your preferred activities.

- **DOG OWNERS.** You are going to have to share your home with a slobbery subservient dog that looks up to humans . . . Are you sure you want this?

- **CAT RESCUERS.** These may be handy if you are between homes, but be very wary about moving in full time. Cat rescuers enjoy rescuing cats so much that you can't call your home your own. There are always newcomers moving in – mangy strays with diseases, flea-ridden alley cats, or heavily pregnant females who will drop a litter of kittens in *your* bed. Cat rescuers seem to think that we, cats, are indiscriminately social like humans are. We are not. We hate all newcomers until we get used to them. We like a stable group of cats without any personnel changes. It may be worth taking up residence for a bit with a cat rescuer if there is nowhere else to go, but move out as soon as you find something better.

Alcohol

This is the human equivalent of catnip. It is drunk rather than sniffed. Sensible humans take it in the same way that we take catnip – in moderation. They may go a bit silly, but not excessively so. However, some humans do not know when they have had enough. They will continue drinking it all evening and some even drink it in the morning. This kind of alcohol user shouts, blunders around, may lose control of its bladder, and may even fall unconscious. If you have a human that does this, rehome yourself.

See also Hangovers

Ankles

A good target area for making your feelings clear.

Artwork

Humans have no appreciation of feline creativity. We leave gloriously scented and carefully designed scratch marks on trees, carpets, walls and furniture. Humans do not even try to appreciate these. Instead, they try to fob us off with rough scratching poles. Ignore these and continue on your lonely creative path. Many true artists are only appreciated after their deaths.

Attention

You will often need to interrupt humans in order to get their attention when they are reading a book, reading online, occupied with social media, tweeting, posting, grooming their face with make-up, sleeping, watching TV, or talking to each other rather than you.

Block their view of the computer by walking on the keyboard. In the case of old-fashioned TV sets, sit on top and let your tail wave about over the screen. Sit on the book or newspaper. Meow loudly. Roll on your back. Jump around wildly. Jump on their laps, shoulders, heads. Throw your-self into their arms. Rub, lick, purr and generally make a fuss of them – most humans will respond with pathetically grateful attention and some of the more stupid ones may believe this is merely affection rather than purposeful interruption.

B is for . . .

Babies

These are the equivalent of kittens and are horribly backward. Their shockingly slow development really shows after the first week. They are helpless for months. Kittens begin to walk at three weeks: babies do not begin walking until they are nine to twelve months old. By twelve weeks, kittens are fully functional and can survive on their own. A twelve-week-old human is completely unable to do anything for itself.

As for developing litter tray use . . . human kittens are hopelessly slow at this. At birth, they leak at both ends. By the age of twelve weeks, kittens have usually established reliable litter tray use. Babies have to wear nappies for months and months, and, even when more or less trained to the human litter tray, will sometimes be unreliable at night.

Kittens are weaned between four to ten weeks: babies have to suckle much longer and are only weaned at four to six months. Our kittens reach puberty from about four months, when the females can start breeding. Human juveniles do not reach puberty until about ten years at the very earliest.

These examples of slow human development show the innate superiority of cats over humans.

See also Sex, Lavatory, Reproduction

Bald

Humans are bald. There may be tiny hairs sparsely dotted about their body, but these are so small and thin that often they are almost invisible. These body hairs (you cannot call them fur) are limp and useless for keeping out the cold. There are patches of thicker fur mostly in the wrong places, such as their armpits and groin, the hot and sweaty areas where hair isn't needed anyway. That's humans for you – badly designed.

True, they have proper fur on their heads, but even this falls out as the males age, and thins in elderly females. Any remaining hair on their heads goes white with age. The lack of head fur is so embarrassing and upsetting for the males, that some middle-aged men shave off all their head hair, preferring total baldness to patchy fur. Others have hair follicles surgically reinserted on their heads or wear false hairpieces.

They would look far more attractive if they had short glossy fur all over their bodies like most cats. Dream about it for a moment. Humans could be furry all over – beautiful black, handsome black and white, sexy striped tabby, gorgeous ginger or tempting tortoise-shell. But they are not. Humans are born naked.

Bathroom – Things to Do There

Don't let your human shut you out of the bath-room. Follow them in. Bathrooms are potential gymnasiums for cats designed for feline fun:

- Catch the drips or drink from the taps in the sink. Drinking water in a bowl can get boring.
- Sit in the sink – a nice smooth circular area for sleeping and very cooling on a hot day. Get your human to upload a photo of this to: www.cats insinks.com.
- Watch for a fish in the lavatory bowl. Most kittens and some cats enjoy watching the water

flush in a lavatory bowl. Maybe, just maybe, they might catch a fish.

- Chase-Your-Tail in the bath at the end furthest from the tap. It works like a fairground wall of death ride. Humans only use the bath to lower their bodies into water. We have more fun without water.
- Paw the bath bubbles. Sit on the side of the bath and poke at the soap bubbles. Or prod any human bits poking out.
- Bat the lavatory paper that hangs down, pulling it out so that the paper spreads all over the floor.
- Enter the shower when the water isn't on. The smell of soap and human is somehow intriguing, and most cats will enjoy rubbing on the shower wall.
- Some cats enjoy playing with the water when their human is using the shower. If you sit just outside and poke your paws inside, you will get damp but not soaked.
- Sleep underneath the heated towel rail, a warm place when the central heating is off.

Beards

In imitation of cats, human males (and some older females) grow whiskers on their chins and round their mouths. It's rather charming to see them wanting to be like us. It doesn't work very well, of course. These human beards are coarser than ordinary fur and very inferior to cats' sensitive whiskers. Still, we appreciate their attempt to make up for hairlessness and some of us enjoy grooming a good human beard. Fragments of food may occasionally be found in a really big beard.

The human envy of our fur reached new heights a few years ago in a frenzy of internet beard-and-cat photos, posing cats in front of the human face, so that it looked as if the feline chin was a human beard. A website called www.cat-beard.com shows the results. Sad.

See also Whiskers

Bed

Sharing your large bed (not the tiny one they bought for you) with a human makes sense. Humans make ideal bed warmers and we cats enjoy heat. What is particularly amusing is the human idea that it is *their* bed. The downside of sleeping with your human is that they take up such a lot of room! Why can't they sleep on the sofa downstairs sometimes? Or on the living-room floor in front of the fire, like we occasionally do?

Here are some useful tips for sharing your bed with humans:

- Get to the bed first and choose the position which suits you. They can fit themselves round you. The middle of the bed is yours. The edges are theirs.
- Insist that they sleep without moving. If you own a couple of humans, discourage any

thought of human romantic activity by walking up the bed, sitting firmly near their heads on the pillow, and staring at them with utter disdain.

- Make sure they do not take up too much room. By gently but firmly leaning against them, you can imperceptibly move them to the edge of the bed without even waking them. When you are in proper control of your humans, of course, you can edge them out of the bed completely, but that would be inhumane. Besides, their distress would interrupt your night's sleep.
- The bottom of the bed is yours on hot nights, when their bodies give out too much heat. Throw your full weight over their toes, which will be withdrawn giving you more space.
- The top of the bed is yours if you enjoy waking and petting your human. A strong purr and some thorough grooming of their head fur will ensure they give you enough space.

- The space between two human bodies is yours during cold nights. Too bad if they want to cuddle: they should have thought of that before they got a cat.
- When they change the sheets, it is fun to wiggle below the bottom sheet, to make a cat-shaped lump.

Birds

Meals on wings for hungry cats. Birdwatching is a good hobby for indoor-only cats, though somewhat frustrating. Helpful humans put out bird tables so that we have a better chance of bagging a bird. For some reason, humans get far more upset about dead birds we bring in than the dead mice. Yet they go out pheasant shooting and slaughter game birds in their thousands, as well as frequently eating chickens. If we are serial killers, so are they. Human inconsistency is fathomless.

Blame

When humans all around you are blaming you,
don't panic. Put on the look of total feline inno-
cence and either stalk away or settle down to
sleep. Yes, maybe you did push over the milk jug
onto the kitchen floor. You are not to blame. It was
their fault for leaving it too close to the edge.
Blame and keep blaming humans. Cats do not
accept blame for anything.

See also Conscience and Guilt

Boxes

A very important part of any cat's life. There's
something irresistible about a cardboard box –
huge boxes, medium boxes and even tiny boxes
that are a squeeze to get into. Sometimes humans
buy them specially for us. They think they are
buying expensive cat toys or equipment. Only

when we ignore the contents and leap into the box, do they realise that the real gift to us is the box itself.

Boxing Day

The only day in the year that humans acknowledge the joy of boxes. And they often leave a few around (left over from the day before) for us to enjoy. If we, cats, had our way, every day would be Boxing Day.

See also Christmas

Burglary

Humans reluctantly acknowledge our talent for this and call successful human burglars 'Cat burglars'. (At least some humans have had the wit to imitate cats.) Burglary and house breaking are part of our skill set. Our agility allows us to enter through top floor windows, sneak over roofs, or drop into basements without making any noise at all. We can steal food under our humans' noses. We enter a larder, eat the remains of the cooked chicken, or steal sausages from a barbecue before humans have noticed. Criminality is a meaningless concept to cats.

Butter

Delicious with or without bread. A fully trained human does not even cut off the area you have licked.

C is for . . .

Cage Birds

Delicious. Thoughtful humans buy them for our entertainment. But beware of parrots. They are big and they bite. They also tease us by imitating human vocalisations.

Caterwauling

Humans do this in the bath or in the shower. They expect us to put up with the noise and sensible cats learn how to ignore this. Caterwauling also emerges from the TV and various other household devices. Sometimes there is a whole choir of humans all caterwauling together. It has been claimed that for cats the most irritating caterwauling human is Justin Bieber. To protect Chinese cats from his caterwauling, the Chinese authorities banned him from performing in the country a few years back. It is ironic that many humans, who enjoy listening to human caterwauling, object when we do it.

Cat Flaps

If your human is intelligent (lucky you) it will get you a private cat flap, which opens only for you and won't let neighbouring cats into your home. Of course, a well-trained human will open doors for you as well, but do not expect the 24-hour service given to Larry the Downing Street cat. A policeman is on duty day and night to open the door for him. Most pet humans cannot offer a

24-hour door service because they have to go out hunting during the day in order to afford our expensive cat food. This is when cat flaps are important, so we can come and go at will.

If only we could microchip humans, we could install a large human flap to keep out all intruders except our own humans. There are some human types we do not want in our homes under any circumstances – vets, vet nurses, doctors (they smell like vets), gamekeepers, adolescent males with airguns, women smelling of dogs, men smelling of dogs, and all children under the age of six.

See also Doors

Catnip

Catnip does nothing for humans. Just as well, perhaps. If they used it, like they use alcohol, there would be none left for us. When humans start sniffing drugs, it is often the beginning of addiction. We do not get addicted to catnip. We are recreational catnip users, not addicts, so there is no need for a Catnip Anonymous.

Cat Shows

Unluckily for us, some humans show cats. They not only want to show us off to competitors, but they want us to win a rosette. Cat shows are unrelieved boredom for us. Hours and hours spent in a cage with humans walking by and impudently staring at you. Nowhere to hide. Not the slightest privacy when you need to use the tiny litter tray. The only break in this torture of dullness is when a weird-looking human comes up and handles you. This is the so-called 'judge'. If you bite it, you will probably never get to a cat show again. Go for a full deep bite and your show career will thankfully be over for good.

Cats That Look Like Hitler

Humans enjoy this website, www.catsthatlooklike
hitler.com, but it is based on a typical human
misunderstanding. Cats don't look like Hitler. It
was Hitler who looked like a cat – a black and
white cat with a black splodge under his nose, to
be precise. In the long term, his feline facial fur
did him no good at all.

Cattery

This is a prison for cats. Small rooms, no carpets,
tiny beds, no sofa for scratching, horrible disinfectant smells and the threatening presence of strange
cats. We cannot escape and sometimes the litter
tray arrangements are inferior, too. Even the most
expensive catteries are a nightmare for most cats.
It is a punishment we don't deserve. And while we
are suffering, our humans are eating themselves
silly and lazing on a sunny beach. Unfair.

Central Heating

One of the few sensible human discoveries in the last ten thousand years of human evolution. Before that, there were open fires, which were better than no heating at all but very smoky. Central heating allows us to lie under the radiator in any room we choose. If your human is mean about heating and turns it off during the daytime, move down the street and look for an elderly person who is in the house all day and can afford good quality food. These are pathetically grateful for your company and often keep their heating on in daytime. You can spend the day with the oldie and then go back to your other home at night.

Chairs

Controlling all important resources – chairs, sofa, beds, bookshelves, etc. – is what we aim for. Even an idle cat can take control of a chair. Take your place there before your human arrives to settle in the same room. Well-trained humans will simply avoid disturbing you. Untrained humans may lift you off the seat, before you have the chance to bite or claw, and sit there in your stead.

Take back control of the chair by waiting till the human leaves – to pour a drink, get a cup of tea, or answer the phone. Jump back quickly and be ostensibly asleep again. If you don't have the patience to wait until the human gets up, jump back on to the chair into a space between your human and the arm of the chair. Settle down. Purr nicely so that your human thinks you are enjoying the closeness. Then slowly edge your way into that space, so that you take it over. Usually within ten minutes, a well-organised cat has taken over at least a third of the space. A further ten minutes and the human is uncomfortably squeezed out.

Christmas

This mid-winter occasion seems to make humans go crazy. They invite strange humans into the house (sometimes with dogs), they drink too much alcohol, eat too much food, and quarrel with each other. Survival tips for the so-called festive period include these:

- On the day itself, spend as much time as you can in the kitchen, where fragments of turkey may fall to the ground.
- Keep an eye on the table; if you are lucky, the bird may be left out unguarded while humans are socialising.
- Launch a full-scale attack at any entering dog, with claws fully protracted while making a large shriek. Do it to them, before they do it to you.
- Give a sharp nip to any strange human who presumes friendship and tries to pet you or pick you up.

- If there are immature human young, don't go near them.
- Take up residence in the bedroom you share with your human – the spare room will be occupied.
- If necessary, spend time under rather than on top of the bed.

Christmas Tree

This is a small fir tree hung with glittering baubles, which are amusing to play with. It is enjoyable to climb up to the top and take the place of the Christmas fairy. Occasionally this brings the tree crashing to the ground and gains instant human attention.

If you get really irritated with Christmas celebrations, pee on the tree.

Clothes

Clothes are the human substitute for fur. Humans feel so bad about being bald, that they cover themselves up with garments. Some humans wear the second-hand fur of other animals, or a look-alike artificial fur in a pathetic attempt to be more like their cat. You have to feel sorry for them.

Colour Prejudice

It is a sad fact that many humans are bigots when it comes to cats. They judge cats by their fur colour, rather than by their temperament or behaviour. Black cats suffer from this prejudice and spend more time in the shelter, trying to find a human who will adopt them.

Brown tortoiseshell cats suffer, too. We cats must work together to end this human colour prejudice.

Computer

Computers are another human obsession that is difficult for our superior species to understand. The little tracks that run across the screen look rather like a mouse's footprint, which may explain human fascination. Humans have named the small plastic device near the keyboard 'a mouse', which of course it isn't. But this symbolic naming may provide a clue to their behaviour. Humans gazing at a computer may be digitally mousing ... you can stop them by simply interposing your body between their eyes and the screen.

See also Keyboard

Concrete – Wet

A great opportunity for artwork. Leave your paw marks for posterity.

Conscience

We don't have one. They do . . . and it can be manipulated in our favour!

See also Guilt

Control

Controlling a human is difficult at times. With their large size, their forceful movements, and their ability to close cupboards and refrigerators, they think they control us. Some things work for us. Our small size means we can hide away from them. Our agile movements mean we can jump, wriggle or run away better than they can.

Cupboards can be manipulated with a paw to see if they will open. Refrigerators are more difficult; we have to work round these by the emotional manipulation of humans. We can also establish coercive feline control using punishment (biting and clawing).

Humans want to be loved by cats. Therefore, one of our punishments is a total refusal to show loving behaviour. Here are some minor punishments which many humans find emotionally upsetting:

- Sleeping in the spare room rather than sharing the bed.
- Refusing to accept stroking.
- Refusing to sit on the lap.
- Refusing to eat what is put down for you. (For obvious reasons this should only be used if you know your human will find some better food.)

- Shunning your human when they arrive home from work.
- Refusing to come in at night when called in at the usual time, meanwhile sitting just out of reach on the garden wall or nearby roof. Add a persistent meow and you will get them really worried.
- Hiding under the bed and refusing to come out.

Curtains

Climbing frames for kittens. Running up the curtains is great exercise for them. It often upsets a human, but why did they put curtains there in the first place? What else are they for? We don't need them. We enjoy looking out into the dark and curtains often get in the way of radiators.

Adding frills to curtains is another kind of artwork. The best method is to take a flying leap halfway up the curtains, stick your front claws in the fabric, and gravity will do the rest. By the time you hit the ground, there will be eight lines of torn material. Two or three leaps and, hey presto, you have frilly curtains!

D is for . . .

Digging

Humans that have gardens dig in them. It's odd to watch, because you expect them to turn round, inspect the hole, and then use it. But they don't. They just keep on digging. Naturally when they have achieved the perfect soil surface for seeds, we use it. And they get extremely angry.

DIY

This is a common way that humans disrupt our territory and, in particular, ruin the safe scent profile of our home. We have spent hours mixing our scent with our humans, then rubbing our chins and cheeks on furniture, doors and skirting boards to get the correct family mix. All this is messed up by humans repainting the house. The noise is appalling. The smell of paint is devastating and our careful work of developing the correct scent profile has to restart from scratch. We may also have to face-rub the skirting boards all over again, if that is where we have left the most important scent messages.

Dogs

These are called 'man's best friend'. That says it all. They have an absurd deference towards humans. They look up at humans as if they were superior beings. Because of this, humans believe them to be loyal and trustworthy, which would be an insult if applied to cats. Canines even let humans train them and seem happy to be trained. It is quite horrible to see a species demean itself in this way. The family dog can be a very bad influence on a human, by giving a human a false sense of its own importance.

The upside is that dogs are easily trained by cats. Start your own obedience classes for a new dog as soon as possible. No messing about with reward training. These are claw-and-order classes – with punishments inflicted where necessary. Do not take any impertinence from a dog. If there is trouble, stand your ground and swipe. Hard. It is essential that you establish your position as Top Cat from the very start of the relationship. The dog must look up to you and accept you as its superior.

Be the family leader. The household hierarchy should go like this: lowest ranking member is the dog; middle ranking member is the human; top rank Alpha is you, the cat.

Domestication

When humans were just hunter-gatherers, they were too primitive to be worth our notice. They wandered around the landscape and built small temporary shelters, rather like tents, made up of branches with animal skins thrown over them. These leaked. They were not at all cat-worthy. Moreover, the Mesolithic humans would uproot them and move off several miles before rebuilding them again. Sometimes they stayed for a few months in caves. These may have been more weatherproof than the skin shelters, but they were still damp and cold. No place for cats.

One animal, the dog, attached itself to humans at this point. It started following the Mesolithic humans in order to eat their waste products. Not only the discarded bones and hide from hunted animals, but also more intimate waste. Poo. Yes, (disgusting as it is) dogs ate poo and that was the foundation for their relationship with men. This is why today's dogs believe that they are part of the human family and are quite happy with the idea of humans being their superiors.

Only when humans settled into proper houses instead of tents or caves did we become interested in them. The main reason was that mice and sparrows moved into human settlements. So, we moved in to hunt the mice and sparrows. As the human species developed, we realised that they had more to offer: they could provide food, warm beds, firesides and so forth. That is when the true process of domesticating humanity started. Once humans recognised our true worth and began worshipping us as goddesses in Ancient Egypt, humans were fully domesticated.

Humans believe they domesticated us – another one of their many extraordinary delusions. We domesticated them. It is true to say that some individual humans are still not entirely domesticated. Their behaviour leaves a lot to be desired.

Doors

These are human-sized cat flaps that swing from the side, rather than the top. Unfortunately, they are usually too heavy for us to open, though some agile cats manage to leap at a door handle and pull it down with their weight. Luckily, humans exist to open the doors for us. Pausing on the threshold, while the human keeps the door open, lets us decide whether to go out or stay in. The decision may take some time.

Teaching humans to open and shut doors for us is relatively easy. The lazier kind of human pet may want to make us use the cat flap (convenient for when they are not in the house), but all cats know that it is more pleasurable to be ushered in and out of the door by a human. The first step in being let out, is to get your human's attention. Some cats, with attentive humans, merely sit by the door waiting to be let out. Others get attention by meowing, rubbing, or even clawing at or biting their human, then walking towards the door.

The noise of meowing will not work as a method of training humans to let you back into the house. Their hearing is so poor, they cannot hear it through the door. However, if the door is made of glass, it is possible to put your front feet on the glass and make exaggerated but silent meows, using your facial muscles. This silent command will often do the trick. Or, stand on your back legs and scrape your front claws down the glass. If all else fails, fling yourself against the door so that it rattles.

Drawers

Agreeable humans often forget to push in the drawers in a chest of drawers. These make a comfy bed among the clean clothes for us. Not quite as good as clean laundry, but similar. Can be a good place to hide, but beware of being shut in by short-sighted humans.

Dressing Up Cats

A horrible human game sometimes practised by young females. A reason for avoiding humans with families. Instant and effective punishment – scratching and biting down hard – is the only way to put a stop to this.

Dustbins

These were once ideal containers for a feline take-away snack. Humans would throw away all kinds of delicacies, such as chicken bones, butter wrapping, fat off a joint, and bits of savoury Yorkshire pudding. A well-built cat could pull down a dust-bin, spreading its contents all over the pavement.

Now these containers have been replaced by large wheeled bins that cannot be turned on their side.

If you are lucky, however, you may live in an area which has small waste bins specifically for food scraps. These can be pulled over and the food reached by biting through the plastic bags, which will then let cats get to the grub. Also keep an eye out for take-away food wrappings that have been thrown out of cars. These often contain interesting chow.

Duties

A good human servant should do the following *every day* without fail:

- Clean the litter box morning and evening.
- Put down fresh 'wet' food morning and evening.
- Renew food in the bowl daily if we are left to feed ourselves *ad lib.*
- Share their meals with us during their meal times.
- Clean feeding bowls and rinse them so that they do not taste of washing-up liquid.
- Put down clean water (away from the food).
- Refresh water bowls every day so that dust does not gather on the surface of the water.
- Groom us, if we are long-haired.
- Open the back door to let us in when required.
- Open the back door to let us out when required.

- Leave enough room (and I mean a minimum of a third of the bed area) for us to sleep during the night.
- Make a bedroom available for us to sleep during the day.
- Put out fresh cat toys so we can have a game at 3 a.m. in the morning.
- Play games with us when required.

E is for . . .

Ears

Human ears are fixed to the side of their heads, so they cannot move them or swivel them. Only about one human in a million can wiggle its ears and, even when they can, they can't wiggle them *directionally*. No wonder they don't hear as well as we do.

Eating

Human eating habits are shameless. Humans get together to have *group* meals. It is embarrassing to watch. They sit in groups round a table *eating*. They have no manners. Feline manners consist of eating, as far as possible, alone. It is the decent thing to do. If we are living in the wild, we go out and catch our own mice, and unless we have kittens, we eat what we hunt. We don't eat in company unless some dumb human insists on feeding us in a row.

Humans also seem unable to eat off the floor. They either sit down and eat off a table, sit in a chair and munch, or walk around with food. This odd way of eating means they are often not aware what has fallen on the floor. Elderly human pets, in particular, may be unable to see what they have dropped. Which means more for us!

More seriously weird is the way they cook (or get somebody else to cook) almost everything they eat. Delicious slices of bleeding meat are transformed into burned grey chunks. Gorgeous juicy chicken legs are turned into dry white legs – still good enough for us to eat, but not as flavoursome as the raw variety. Feathers and hide are always taken off their food, so there is no chance to tear and pluck, part of our natural feeding repertoire that enhances our eating experience.

For some odd reason, if we use our paw to investigate and eat food out of our bowl, humans think this is very clever. Try it. They will probably start filming you for YouTube.

Emotionally Needy Humans

Humans who are too emotionally dependent on their cat do not make good pets. This kind of human is demanding, clingy, insecure and always looking for feline validation. It is over-sensitive to any feline failure to fulfil their needs, but may be totally insensitive to *our* own needs. Human neediness shows itself in unwanted petting, constant picking up, and repeated cuddling.

Walk away. You are not there to fulfill their need for reassurance. You have a life to lead without human harassment or interference.

Energy Conservation

Humans waste a lot of time doing things. When in doubt we nap. They would be happier if they did the same.

Evolution – Human

Any investigation of evolution shows that cats have ascended to the top of the tree of life, while humans are a mere naked side-shoot of the monkey family. We, cats, are the master species, but strangely enough humans suffer from delusions of grandeur. This occurs because they value technology over serenity.

Humans may have done boring stuff like inventing the wheel or landing on the moon, but we have had a really good time mousing and sleeping in the sun for thousands of years. Which is the wisest species? It doesn't always pay to be a smartie. Who gets the free cat food? Not dumb humans. They have to work for theirs.

Moreover, humans are now fatally dependent upon a wide variety of expensive resources. We need food and shelter. And some mice. Humans need houses with separate bedrooms, furniture, bottles, plates, bricks and mortar, cash, bank accounts, cars, petrol, wood burning stoves, water heaters, electricity, gas, coal, computers, TVs, electric shavers, flushing lavatories, hair curlers, books, boots, high-heeled shoes, gloves, hats, and handbags.

Take a look through your local rubbish dump (also a good place for mousing), if you want to get a true picture of this dysfunctional species.

Eyeballing Your Human

Use the command stare. The feline stare can be intimidating for some humans, who consider it giving the evil eye. Use this weakness for your own advantage. A hard stare, combined with a lashing tail and swivelled-back ears, may make biting unnecessary. It is always good to avoid violence.

Use your eyes to communicate with your humans in gentler ways, too. Some of the more intelligent humans learn to follow our gaze. Looking at the human then transferring that gaze to the fridge or food cupboard may help them understand you require food. The friendly steady stare before jumping on a lap prepares them for the impact.

Finally, there is the slow blink. Really clever humans, and there aren't many of these, recognise this as a message of love.

Eyesight

Humans can't see in the dark and their vision is not reliable in the twilight. They are daylight animals. They light up their houses when night falls and stay awake in artificial light. This accounts for their huge electrical bills. They miss all the excitement of a twilight and night time world – the hoot of the owl, the sleepy cheep of a bird in the hedgerow, the footfall of a passing predatory fox and – best of all – the rustle of a field mouse in the grass. This is the world of the twilight hunter and humans spoil it all by turning on street lights. Idiots.

F is for . . .

Fat Cats

An offensive term applied to rich humans. Cats consider this a prejudicial term of abuse showing innate human speciesism. It should be banned as a politically incorrect hate crime. Immediately.

Feet

They have only two of them. And their feet are weird – no retractable claws, simply nails that lie there unable to move independently. No sensitive fur between the toes. They cannot use their feet to scratch themselves or to hold themselves up when climbing trees. No scent glands on the big pad at the bottom, though there is quite an interesting individual scent left on old socks. And, of course, if they stumble, they fall over, as they don't have three other legs to keep themselves upright. As the old saying goes: 'Four feet good: two feet bad.'

Female Humans

To give human females their due, they do try to be clean, even if it involves an enormous waste of water, rather than simply using their tongues. Most of them wash daily. Then what happens next is really odd. They apply oils, pastes and creams to their skin. They paint their lips red, their eyelids blue, and even put black paste on their eyelashes. The scent of these is overpowering, although because they have a bad sense of smell, they are immune to it. These unguents and oils seem to be a substitute for the saliva-scent that we apply with our tongues to our fur. Human males are beginning to copy this female behaviour.

See Nose Blind

Feral Humans

These are humans that are poorly adapted to domestication. Juvenile ferals, usually in groups, may throw stones at us, fire air guns at us, chase us with dogs, or even throw us into bonfires on Guy Fawkes' night or Halloween. Feral humans can be very dangerous indeed. Keep clear of them.

The typical feral is a male wearing a hoodie, with tattoos, body piercings, boots, leather garments, and with a pit bull terrier straining on a leash. It (the human as well as the dog) often makes snarling or shouting vocalisations. If the dog has scars on its face, it may be a professional canine fighter, whose early training included killing cats. These ferals have guns and knives instead of claws. Feral females, with the tattoos, leather and boots, and snarling dogs, are also occasionally sighted. Keep clear of these, too.

Can ferals be tamed? Most cats believe that their wild human nature cannot be changed, though a few cats have succeeded in taming a feral human. But why bother?

Fingers and Thumbs

If we had these, we would rule the world and it would be a much better place. Except for mice.

Fish

Fresh fish can be very tasty. Go fishing at nearby garden ponds for goldfish. With luck, you may even find you can land a gigantic Koi carp. These are awesomely large, but beware of their owners. For some reason, humans get very distressed and very angry if they see you whisking over the garden fence with one of these in your mouth. Thoughtful humans sometimes supply indoor goldfish or tropical fish in a tank for us. It is always good to go fishing.

See also Goldfish

Flies

When no other prey is available, flies can help stave off boredom. For indoor-only cats, they may provide the only possible hunting opportunity. They also make a satisfying crunchy snack. Curiously, humans get upset when we kill butterflies, but are perfectly fine about house flies or cockroaches. They are particularly likely to laugh when we try to catch a fly walking across the TV screen.

Night hunting, when you pursue a fly or a moth over the bodies of your sleeping humans, is particularly good fun. If you are lucky, you may find a cockroach to drop on their pillow.

Food – Theirs

Humans feast on a wide variety of food, while we get the same food daily. No wonder that we haunt kitchen surfaces in search of variety. The following tips may be helpful:

• Train your human to share its meal with you. Use the correct body language – tilted head, expressively imploring eyes, and a gentle rubbing of your head against the ankles. Add a little cry into your strongest purring. The cry within the purr makes it clear that you are soliciting food, rather than merely expressing happiness.

- Sit on the table close to its plate and stare at each portion of food moving on its fork or spoon towards its mouth.
- If your gaze doesn't do the trick, snag the food off the fork with a gentle paw. This is best done when a human is on its own: they are embarrassed to be seen by other humans when they are sharing food with cats.
- Sit on the kitchen surfaces close to a human when it is preparing a meal. Best time is when the human is slicing or stirring. Use your gaze to show how hungry you are. A tiny imploring meow may also help.
- Scan the floor in all rooms where food is prepared or eaten. Some crumbs will always fall.
- Keep a sharp eye on kitchen cupboards. Absent-minded humans sometimes forget to shut away food.

Humans have odd food fads about what they will eat. Some insist they are herbivores and won't eat any kind of meat or fish. Most will refuse to eat insects. For obvious reasons, try to choose a meat-eating pet.

Food – Ours

Teaching humans how to buy the correct food is difficult. We cannot accompany them to the super-market and *show* them what kind of food to buy. We have to train them at a distance to purchase the correct brand. This requires a considerable effort around the food bowl.

Remember to be consistent and patient with this inferior species. The wrong food must not be eaten. Walk up to the food bowl. Sniff. Look down at the food. Turn to your human, look distressed and mew plaintively. Sniff again, then stalk away. Or if this doesn't work, consider scraping round the food bowl, as if you were burying something in the litter tray. The message to your human is: 'This is s***, so I am burying it.'

Most humans weaken at this behaviour and will offer something better. If they don't and you are so hungry that you need to eat, then eat slowly and disdainfully. Picking up each portion and shaking it, as if disgusted by what is on offer. Do not finish up inferior food and never, ever, lick the bowl. If the food is good, or an interesting new flavour, purr loudly while your mouth is full. Even dumb humans know that it shows your pleasure.

If all else fails, check out neighbouring cat flaps and steal other cats' food.

Fur Envy

The most obvious reason for cat superiority is our fur. Humans feel their inferiority in the matter of fur. This results in subconscious *fur envy*, according to cat psychoanalysts. How do they come to this conclusion? Human behaviour is so strange, that only a strong mental complex such as fur envy explains it.

Caring cats sometimes try to reduce human alopecia by adding their fur to their human. It sticks best to their clothing, rather than their naked flesh. Transferring our hair is also a form of artwork – gleaming feline fur makes lovely patterns on dark human clothing and also transmits a reassuring family scent. These efforts are not appreciated by your human. We don't know why.

See also Hair

Furniture

The best furniture is designed for felines to exercise their claws. There is nothing more satisfying than a well-upholstered sofa or armchair when it comes to upright scratching. These offer enough height and stability for a really satisfying downward scratch. For those of us who prefer a horizontal scratch, carpet is also satisfying. Some cats also swear by table legs and wallpaper. Hopeful humans offer so-called scratching posts, but these come a poor second to good furniture.

Most cats scratch the back and the arms of the armchairs, but do not forget the front area. If you stand on the chair seat itself, you can get a good downward scratch. Soon the whole chair will be decorated with frilly threads. It makes a lovely sight and a satisfying texture when you update the grooves. Humans sometimes buy 'distressed' mohair or leather, so as to give their surroundings an antique look. Now you can do it for them – chair legs, chair backs, tables, rugs, carpet, and wooden doors. We can 'distress' all of these.

G is for . . .

Garden

Humans should supply the following in their garden:

- Hiding places in long grass and tall plants.
- Look-out places on high fences, walls, or garden furniture.
- Trees or logs to scratch on.
- No horrible smelling chemical sprays or slug bait.
- A bird table for bird-watching and for outdoor snacking.
- Catnip and other catmint species where we can hang out, tune in and drop out for few minutes.
- Sunny spots for a nap.
- Some shelter from wind or rain – a cat flap into the garden shed would be nice.
- A garden pond for drinking rainwater, instead of chemical tasting tap water.
- Garden ponds are good for a takeaway fish snack. On sunny idle days, it is lovely to watch fish or sit in mindful contemplation of the

universe. An outside bowl for rain water will do if there isn't a pond.

- An outside latrine. Think seedbeds, newly dug flower beds, shredded bark, peat, compost, builder's sand, a children's sand pit, or even fine gravel. If it is not supplied in your garden, visit a neighbour's garden.

Gifts *from* Humans

Humans enjoy giving gifts to their cats, but accepting human gifts puts you in debt to this inferior species. Beware of bribes. They compromise your independence. Here are the rules about accepting gifts:

- Expensive gifts should be ignored.
- Large gifts should be ignored in favour of the box they came in.
- Toys should be ignored in favour of playing with small items like paper clips, biros, pieces of dry pasta, papers, string, rubber bands, etc.

- If you really want to accept a gift, wait a few months. Only start using it or playing with it when you hear them discussing whether to give it away.
- The only exception is food. Food should always be accepted, even if you are not hungry, especially food from a human plate. It encourages the human to continue to share their food.

Gifts *to* Humans

Humans are without gratitude. Presented with a juicy fat mouse or a struggling baby rat, they will often scream, jump on chairs, or try to push you back outside. Worse still, they may take this delicious item off you and 'set it free'.

See also Mice

Goldfish

Humans go fishing, but they don't like it when we do. It is almost too easy to scoop goldfish out of their tank, but you risk falling in if you have to balance on the edge of it. Idle cats, who can't be bothered to pull out the fish, can treat the tank like a feline TV.

Grooming

Humans cannot reach the most important places with their floppy tongues and soft nails. They also lack those little front teeth that allow us to pull out dead fur, or chase down a flea. Instead, they regularly pour water on their heads to shampoo and rinse their fur. This destroys any natural oils or scents.

In view of their lack of grooming ability, should we help them out? Let's get one thing straight at the start. We can't groom a human properly. There is obviously too much of them. They present a huge ungroomed area, most of it hidden by clothes. It is not our job to clean them thoroughly. If that is our aim, we are bound to fail, and we may have a nervous breakdown trying.

You can do a little helpful grooming by sitting on the back of an armchair or sofa, placing a firm paw on the head and nibbling at the fur on their heads. Some cats also claim that licking a human's bald head may make its hair grow back. Very few humans enjoy this, but some cats are conscientious about keeping their humans clean, so purrsist.

Guilt

We do not do guilt. They do. Make human guilt work in your favour.

Habits – Irritating Human

Irritating human habits are difficult to cure. A sensible cat learns that what cannot be cured must be ignored, though sometimes it is hard. These are some of them:

- Turning over in bed while we are trying to sleep at night.
- Refusing to share their food with us, so we have to steal it.
- Fidgeting while we are asleep on their knees. Why can't they sit still?
- Incessant vocalising to us in a high-pitched friendly tone. Obviously, they are trying, though failing, to communicate. But what does 'Blah . . . blah . . . blah' mean?
- Failure to clean the litter tray frequently enough. Cleaning immediately after use would be ideal, though many cats settle for twice a day.

- Slow meal service. We shouldn't have to remind them by winding round their legs.
- Failure to open doors, so that we have to squeeze through the cat flap.

Hair

Humans are embarrassed by their lack of hair. They fuss around the tufts on their head. They brush, comb, fluff it out, cut, shave it all off, dye, wash and condition it. The males spend hundreds of pounds on replanting little tufts in amusing lines, or buying false fur toupees to fill in the top bald area. The rich females buy hair from poor females and tie it to their own hair to make it look thicker and longer.

Meanwhile they are busy reducing the hair anywhere else. The females shave off the tufts under their armpits and shape the hair around their groin area into strange patterns. They also shave off all the tiny hairs on their legs. The males trim the hair in their nose and ears. While many men keep their chest fur, a recent trend among them has been to shave it off. Odd.

See also Bald, Beards and Fur Envy

Hamster

A delicious little snack if you can get it out of its cage. They are also great fun to watch throughout the night, though it is frustrating not to be able to put your paws through the bars of their cage. Humans often buy a hamster for us, but then will not let us hunt it down. However, do not put your nose too near the bars, as they bite quite severely.

Handbags

An excellent place to stash that dead mouse. Your human will cry out with delighted surprise when she finds it.

Hangover

Humans who drink too much alcohol suffer from this syndrome. They sweat, they are restless in bed, they utter low groans while placing their hand to their forehead, and they find it difficult to eat breakfast. Instead they drink a lot of coffee. It is sad to see them in this pathetic condition. While the human is still in the bed, walk up closely and purr loudly down its ear. It is the loving thing to do.

Harassment

Humans often harass us for affection. They interrupt our sleep with forcible petting. They insist on stroking us for hours. They try to tickle our bellies. They lift us off the ground and put their faces too close to us, ruffling our whiskers. They give horrible squeezing hugs. They give even more horrible cuddles. At best, we lose our poise and dignity. At worst, it is very upsetting.

Stiffen your body to show how much you dislike their maladroit efforts at affection. A completely rigid body may be enough to make them put us down. If not, claw and bite.

Hearing

Deafness is another human disability. We can hear a mouse's tiny squeak, or the rustle of its footfall. They cannot hear mice even when these are in their own house. You have only to sit in their living room with the TV blaring out to realise how deaf they are compared to us.

See also Nose Blind

Hiding Places

If humans cannot *see* us, they cannot find us. They cannot track us down by scent, as their noses barely work at all. Good hiding places are essential for all cats. We need them for when the dreaded 'vet' word is overheard, and for any time suitcases are in evidence. Try hiding in the following places:

- The seat of a chair that is pushed under the table.
- Top of the wardrobe.
- Bottom of the wardrobe behind the shoes and clothes.
- Behind the sofa.
- In the covered litter tray.
- Between the washing machine and the boots in the utility room.
- Under the spare room bed.
- Behind the fridge.
- Inside a suitcase.
- Inside an open drawer.

Hoarders

Beware of taking cat food from strangers. They may seek to kidnap you. Some humans have become addicted to cats and cannot resist snatching up any passing feline. If you are not careful, they will lure you into their house and then not let you out again. Inside is feline hell. The house is filled with scores of cats, not enough litter trays, not enough food, and often with diseased and dying kittens. These humans are seriously mad.

If you are thinking of rehoming yourself to a friendly stranger, check that there is a cat flap so you can leave when you want. If there isn't one, check at the windows before entering the house. If more than one cat is sitting at the window looking out, this may be a hoarder household. Proceed with great caution.

Holidays and Vacations

Once or twice a year, humans leave their homes and vanish. This is usually a deeply unpleasant experience for cats. Their absence wouldn't be too bad, except that we still miss the comforts of our own particular pet – the comfortable lap, the occasional treat from their plate, the warm body sleeping in our bed upstairs.

Sometimes a relative or a stranger invades our home in order to feed us. This can work out well if the new human is tuned into cats and is willing to share our bed. It can be very stressful if the relative is not a cat lover. At other times, it will be one of the neighbours who comes in once or twice a day to put down food.

Worst of all is when they put us into prison during their so-called 'holiday'. This is usually a pen with unfamiliar smells, the noise and scents of other strange cats, and an inadequate litter tray. There is nothing to do except stare out through the wire. It is even worse for rescue cats, as it brings back the feelings of abandonment when they were stuck in a shelter trying to adopt a human.

What can we do about it? Keep a sharp eye on the human's suitcases. If these are taken out of the cupboard, this may mean a 'holiday' is looming. Also tune your ears to their vocal chattering in case you hear the word 'cattery'.

Take your revenge when you return from your prison sentence. Cower and refuse to be picked up by your human, making it look as if you are terrified. Once at home, refuse to have anything to do with your humans for at least three days.

See also Cattery

Homo Sapiens

They call themselves *Homo sapiens*, which is Latin for Wise Man. Any sensible feline knows that they are nothing of the kind. So why the name? The answer, sadly, is that humans invented this name for themselves. This species thinks that it is intelligent. Even odder, humans believe that they, alone of all the animals, can make good choices. This is perhaps the biggest human delusion. Humans are making the planet uninhabitable for many other creatures by trashing the oceans with plastic, forcing up the temperature of the planet by burning fossil fuels, and melting the ice cap so that sea levels are rising dangerously.

A quick look at human history with its wars and famines makes clear the madness of believing that humans are wise. No reasonable animal slaughters millions of its own species. No rational animal goes to war. Sure, animals sometimes fight each other, but most of those fights are organised in a way that means nobody gets killed. And no animal in the whole history of the world (except humans) has ever invented weapons to slaughter thousands of its own species.

They have wiped out many of the large mammals like mammoths and continue to slaughter, hunt and kill elephants, big cats, and bears. Their agriculture is eroding the soil, devastating insect life, and exterminating wild flowers. *Homo sapiens?* We don't think so.

However, tamed and trained, they are not all bad. They make good pets, buy us cat food so we don't go hungry, supply warm housing, and are really quite cute in a clumsy kind of way.

Hunting

There are a few humans who hunt – in a very unsporting way. Instead of tracking, pouncing and eating their prey with their own efforts, they cheat. They will use a pack of dogs to do their tracking for them, and horses to help the pursuit. Or they finish off their game at a distance using a gun. *Usually they don't eat it.*

Humans criticise us for catching mice when we are fed up with cat food. Frankly, this is what human hunters do. The hypocrisy is shocking. They say we hunt too many birds. Yet in country areas, humans will specially raise thousands of game birds in pens, put them out into the wild, and then slaughter them in their hundreds with guns. We, cats, would have too much pride to behave like this.

Most humans do not hunt at all. They forage for food that has been hunted down by somebody else. They call it shopping. I was told by a cat, who lived near Tesco's, that humans would stream into this huge warehouse and come out laden with food. There was so much food that a lot of it got thrown away. He used to hang round near the supermarket dustbins and said you could live off human leavings very easily – though it was cold there under the bins.

Strangely, humans also forage for stuff they can't eat – clothes to cover their nakedness, mobile phones, flowers (not edible ones), electric toasters (useful for toasting mice), pictures to hang on the wall, bicycles, towels, paperclips . . . they bring home quantities of *pointless stuff.*

I is for . . .

Ice Cream

Cold but delicious. It is the fat in the ice cream, not the sweetness, that is so moreish. If your human is eating ice cream, purrsuade them to give you a lick. Ice cream containers and wrapping should be pulled out of the trash can and given a thorough cleaning.

Ignoring a Human

Humans rapidly become dependent upon our approval. Which is odd, when you consider that they admire our independence. Test this out for yourself. Spend an evening without purring or rubbing on your human. Ignore it as much as possible. Sit with your back to it. Refuse all eye contact. You will see that the human becomes anxious, even depressed. You have discovered a secret method of manipulation. It may well result in a desperately worried human offering food. Ignoring is also an effective feline punishment.

Indoors Lifestyle – Cats

Those of us cats who have an indoor-only lifestyle, but allow our humans to come and go, must be creative in our activities. Indoor sports include hunting flies, cockroaches and other insects; using lavatory paper as a scratching post; drinking from a dripping tap; climbing curtains; clearing small items off mantlepieces, counters and tables; watching TV and investigating if wildlife is hiding behind the set; exercising our paws on the computer keyboard; pulling socks out of drawers; playing hunt-the-human-toes; drug-sniffing catnip toys; and, of course, sleeping all over the place.

Play with your human as much as possible by hunting them like a mouse. They may object, but they enjoy it really.

See also Play.

Indoors Lifestyle – Human

Most of us keep our humans with free access to come and go from the house, but there are a growing number who feel that humans should be indoor-only pets. The indoor-only human is available to feed us, stroke us, or share sleep with us twenty-four hours a day. Humans that are currently indoors most of the time include the lazy, the elderly, the sick and those that are both extremely obese and extremely comfortable to sleep on. Evolution may be playing a part here – evolving humans in order to suit cats.

Intelligence

Human intelligence has been much over-rated – by humans, of course. They have a certain ingenuity, but this does not make up for the fact that they think in an unnecessarily weird way. They have higher order thinking. This over-think makes them categorise things, invent patterns in life, and have imaginary and abstract concepts, such as 'politics', 'morals', 'logic', 'judgement', 'philosophy', 'string theory', 'metaphysics', and 'zero point energy'. Most of these concepts make them miserable instead of happy, so it is difficult to see any advantage in this kind of thought.

In comparison, we cats are as clever as we need to be. Humans cannot compete with us when it comes to hunting rodents, leaving interesting scent messages for other cats, being able to live a solitary life if we choose, and rehoming ourselves when our current living arrangements are not to our choosing. We don't let abstract stuff in our heads make us unhappy.

Internet

This is our new domain. We dominate the digital world. We have taken over YouTube, Instagram,

Facebook, and almost all other digital areas. By 2015, there were two million YouTube videos of cats, which had been watched 25 million times. By now there are millions more views and millions more photos of us on Instagram and Facebook.

The internet has been described as 'a virtual cat park, a social space for cat lovers in the same way that dog lovers congregate at a dog park'. Today there is an annual internet cat video festival and cat pictures are posted more often than selfies.

When Google developed an artificial brain, naturally the first thing it did was to browse YouTube to look for cats. It managed a 74.8 per cent accuracy in recognising them. A few years later, Google's artificially intelligent camera, CLIPS, was particularly good at capturing our cute moments. Humans did not foresee this feline domination of the digital world.

The human creator of the web, Sir Tim Berners-Lee, was asked if there was anything he could not have predicted about the internet. He replied: 'Kittens.' But it was obvious to us.

There are now thousands of cats that blog or tweet directly, like I do. Admittedly, we have to depend on human hands to type in our messages to the world, but most humans seem willing to do this. There is even a cat blogosphere website: https://blog.catblogosphere.com/. Join us in the digisphere.

See World Domination

J is for . . .

Jigsaws

If you are lucky, your human will buy a jigsaw: a box of small, oddly shaped wooden tablets. Humans empty the box, and when small pieces fall out, they spend hours trying to fit them together. This can be fun for cats, too. The pieces are lightweight and make good toys for batting around. It is also fun to knock a completed jigsaw off the table and rearrange the pieces on the floor.

Jokes

Before playing a joke with your human, remember that they have a poor sense of humour. Jokes include: rolling on your back as if to invite a belly rub, then sticking all eighteen claws into their hand; pushing glasses of water off the bedside cabinet; jumping into the lavatory basin; and running up curtains. But humans quite often fail to see the funny side.

See also Trees

Jumping Up High

Another example of human inferiority. Humans cannot jump like we do. A male human can jump about 16–19 inches vertically from a standing position. This is a pretty low jump, when you consider that a male human can be six feet high. A cat can jump 108 inches high, about ten times its own height.

Jumping up high is not only a way to escape dogs and feral humans: it is also a good way of asserting your superiority. As you gaze down on the human below, you are reminding them that they are an inferior species. It is sometimes called 'the moral high ground'. Humans can only do this metaphorically. We can do it for real.

K is for . . .

Keyboard

A place to sleep. Though not very comfortable, it is slightly warm and has a nice smell from human fingers. Alternatively, you can stand upon or walk across the keyboard. Interesting little mouse tracks can be seen when we put our weight on it. As a creative exercise, this does not have the same satisfaction for us as artwork on wallpaper or furniture. However, it is an excellent way of getting human attention.

Kibble – Dried Food

Humans spend a few seconds pouring kibble into our bowl and then spend hours in the kitchen cooking up delicious and varied meals for themselves. We are expected to eat the same dried pellets every single day, while they feast on tasty different dishes of fish, meat, and chicken.

No wonder we steal human food. It is the only way to have a change of diet.

Kitchen Counters

There is a rather pathetic 'rule' invented by humans that cats should not walk upon kitchen counters. Take not the slightest notice. Kitchen counters have interesting scraps of food, half open packets and open tins of edible substances, and (if we are quick and we are) we can sometimes use a paw to snatch a pork chop out of the frying pan.

This rule was made to be broken. It is important that you start the way you go on: i.e., walk on the counters as often as you choose. Humans move from exasperation through mild annoyance to total acceptance of our right to be there. It is rather sweet to see that psychological journey. After about three to six months, humans will drop the rule.

Kitchen Paper Rolls

These provide a paper chase for indoor cats. Like lavatory paper rolls, only larger. Get your claws into them and tug.

Knees – Human

Bony human joints that protrude when sitting, allowing a useful area for sleep. Fat humans have softer knees and older humans are likely to sit immobile for longer. These knees are the best for sitting.

See also Laps

L is for . . .

Laps

Humans, desperate for feline love, love it when cats sleep on their laps. Jumping on a lap is a good way to get adopted, as the human feels specially chosen. But some of us do not wish to sit on laps, particularly if the knees are thin and boney. Some humans harass us by picking us up and placing us on their knee. If they do this, always move off smartly. It is important that lap sitting should be entirely voluntary.

Laps can be pleasant at times, particularly if the central heating is not on high enough. Human warmth combines with feline warmth to make a cosy spot. Much depends on the ability of the human to stay still. Avoid the lap if your human is liable to fidget or persists in stroking for too long. Most of us want to sleep quietly on laps and resent being woken up every five minutes or so.

Lap Cats

A potentially demeaning term applied by humans to cats that unselfishly please their humans by sitting on their laps. Some of us do not feel comfortable there. Others feel that it is below their dignity to honour human laps. Wanting all cats to be 'lap cats' is another example of human selfishness.

Laughter

Humans make a curious vocalisation when they find life amusing. Be resilient about this. Of course, it is irritating that humans see us as figures of fun, but that is part of their limited intelligence. Instead, make laughter work *for* you. If you are bored and need human stimulation, do something that will make them laugh. It never fails to get their attention. Possibilities include:

- Standing on your hind legs.
- Pouncing on paper clips.
- Leaping high into the air.
- Teasing a friendly family dog.
- Sitting on the human's head.
- Growling at big cats on TV.
- Stealing socks.
- Sleeping somewhere odd like inside a very small cardboard box, in a waste paper basket, or on top of the microwave.
- Pushing a full glass of water off the kitchen table.
- Sitting upright like a human with your back against the sofa and your legs flung out.
- Attacking a mirror.
- Drinking from a dripping tap.
- Hanging from a chandelier.
- Poking at the TV screen.

Laundry – Fresh

Humans provide this for us on a regular basis. Is it the smell or the texture? I cannot make up my own mind about which of these is more enticing. But there is no finer sleeping place than a heap of freshly ironed laundry.

Lavatory – The Human Litter Tray

Nobody has taught humans how to use a litter tray. They do not understand about digging and burying their waste products in the hygienic way that we felines use. Instead they squat upon a large drinking bowl, do their business, and then flush it away with water. We cannot read the minds of lower animals like humans, but I think it is safe to assume that humans feel some of the same satisfaction as we do with a Job Well Done.

Lavatories are useful for cats that like being stroked but not picked up. You can trap your human on the lavatory bowl, when you require some petting. Once installed on the lavatory, the sitting human cannot move away. If you wind yourself around its legs, it is almost bound to bend down and pet you – without any nonsense about picking you up and placing you on a lap.

Some of us also enjoy drinking from the lavatory, or observing the flush of water in the hope that a goldfish or two might turn up in the pan. They never do, but for a bored cat, the bubbles are fun to watch.

Legs

Humans have half the number of legs that we have. They are bipeds, while we are quadrupeds. Walking on two legs makes balancing difficult. Human babies have to crawl along using their knees and hands in order not to injure themselves by falling off their legs. The very young ones and the very old ones are unsteady on their feet, and even the adolescents fall over on a Saturday night after too much alcohol, their substitute for catnip.

Litter Tray

Trying to explain to your human that the litter box is not clean enough can be difficult. But here are a few ideas:

- Wait till they clean the box, then nip inside and use it. *Message – I like a clean litter box.*
- Pee inside, then poo somewhere else in the house. *Message – I want a second litter box, one for pee and one for poo.*
- Stop using the litter box altogether. *Message – not enough litter, the wrong litter, the wrong location, or I don't like this particular box any more. Do something fast.*

 is for . . .

Mantlepiece

This is the shelf that is found above a fireplace. It is usually cluttered with small items such as cards, photos, scented candles, china ornaments, invitations, and all kinds of odds and ends. At times there may also be half-drunk glasses of wine or cups of tea. Sometimes even champagne glasses. All this human stuff is in our way.

We can avoid these objects when we jump up on to a mantlepiece and unerringly pick our way through them without their falling off the shelf. But why should we? It is more fun to push them off. Keep an eye on your humans, to make sure they are looking at you, tap the item thoughtfully and then deliberately shove it off. Champagne glasses make a delightful tinkling noise as they smash.

Meowing – Ours

We don't meow much between ourselves. We are relatively silent animals and we save our meows for baby-talk to kittens. But the language of the meow (and of the purr) is one that humans can understand. As vocal animals, they respond to a good meow and even begin to get the message. Some of the more intelligent humans even begin to understand what we are saying – though it may take months or even years.

If we are consistent and patient, we can train them by meowing to open cupboards, or even to give us a slice of turkey from their plate.

Mice

We have tried. We have really tried. We have presented live mice, dead mice, half-dead mice, and bits of half-eaten mice. This should be ideal finger food for a hungry human. But humans will NOT eat a mouse, even though the crunchy tail is not unlike pork crackling, which they consume with enthusiasm.

Really devoted cats will often tempt their human by bringing in a positive buffet of prey through the cat flap – young rats, baby rabbits, the occasional small snake, frogs, or even fish from the neighbour's pond. We know that some humans eat frogs, rabbits and carp, but they refuse to eat what we provide. Humans have no gratitude. It is a hopeless task.

Some of us even try teaching them to hunt mice by bringing these in alive. Humans release captive animals into the wild: we release mice into captivity in the house. That is how we train our kittens, and because humans have the intelligence of a retarded kitten, we believe this might work. But it doesn't. No matter how hard we try, they usually respond by shrieking and running. This reaction is quite amusing to watch.

So where is the best place to stash a living mouse, so that we can hunt it at 3 a.m. in the morning? Or a dead mouse so that we can play with it in the early hours? I suggest the following places. Some are best for dead mice: others for living ones. Some work for both:

- Under the bed.
- Behind the living-room sofa.
- Inside a bedroom slipper.
- In a handbag.
- Behind the microwave on the kitchen counter.
- In a paper file.
- Inside a Wellington boot.
- Underneath the fridge.
- On top of the kitchen table next to the salt and paper cruets.
- On the doormat.

- Inside the toaster if it is dead, so that the human can toast it when it is getting its breakfast.

Microchip

If only we could microchip our humans. There are now microchip-operated cat flaps: why are there no microchip-operated human doors? We could adapt our front and back door so that it only opened when our own humans came in. That would stop unwanted visitors. Humans would also be safe from burglars. They clearly aren't intelligent enough to see the advantages.

Mine – The Cat Motto

What's mine is mine and what's yours is mine, too.
As all cats know, what is theirs, is ours. Their human bed is ours. Their armchair is ours. Their food is ours (if they are not looking). Their radiators are ours. As for the stuff they buy for us, those expensive cat trees, new bowls, special cat blankets, and costly cat toys . . . we don't want them anyway.

Mobile Phone

Humans are obsessed with these curious rectangular gadgets. These emit vocal noises, sometimes even tempting bird songs or mouse squeaks. There are also moving pictures and strange little marks on a screen, like those on the computer.

Most of these, apart from the bird and rodent noises, are of no feline interest.

Humans carry these gadgets around and seem almost addicted to them, unable to notice what is going on around them. Every time the gadget emits a noise, they stick the gadget close to one ear to enhance the sound. They walk around all day in this uncomfortable position, unable to hear anything else. They risk life and limb by this obsession, as they cannot pause to avoid obstacles or even cars. They vocalise incessantly into them.

Occasionally, a strategically placed paw on the phone will make it light up, or change the moving pictures. Humans can become very excited when we show an interest, or pretend to show an interest, in the pictures. A simpler way to get human attention is by pushing these off the table or pretending to pounce on them.

Moonlight

Our eyes reflect moonlight, but human eyes are dull at night. Our human pets don't have that reflective layer of shining cells that mirrors the light from other sources like the moon or car lights. Maybe that is why they don't understand that moonlight is for hunting, not for romance. They miss all the fun of a new moon – the squeaks in the hedgerows, the hoot of a hunting owl, the rustle of a hedgehog, the grunts of a badger, and the sight of the grazing deer that come out when humans go to bed.

Mouse

The same humans that refuse our gifts of a mouse, pretend that a plastic device on a string is a mouse. Envy? Sheer stupidity? Many of us have poked this plastic, so-called mouse, but nothing interesting happened, except for leaving more of

their footprints upon the computer screen.
Pointless? Not altogether. If you pretend this is a
real mouse and pounce on it, this makes most
humans laugh. It is hard to understand why.

 is for . . .

Names

We recognise the names humans give us. We know if they use our name that they would like us to come when called. But we take no notice. It is important not to let humans get the idea that they can give us commands.

Humans, however, do *not* recognise the names we give them, probably because we call them by their personal scent. Their signature-smell names cannot be written here, of course, but every cat will know what I mean. We identify friend and foe by individual scent. Indeed, because their sense of smell is so limited, and humans only recognise very strong smells, they might even be offended if they knew their signature-scent name was something like 'Aftershave-Beer-Smelly Socks'.

Naps

The gift of napping is something humans do not have. We can nap anytime, anywhere. Most humans wait till it is getting dark to sleep and then go on sleeping until it starts getting light. They miss the pleasures of midnight prowling, of hunting by the light of the moon, or walking home in the dawn. Some of the oldies start napping in front of their TV in the evening, but none of them seem to understand that twilight, night and dawn are for activity, while midday is for sleep. Only in Spain do humans understand the pleasurable necessity of a siesta.

Neutering – If Only

Humans would be so much happier if they were neutered at an early age. They wouldn't know what they were missing. While they are perfectly happy to give us the snip, they are extraordinarily reluctant to do this to themselves. If it is good enough for cats, it should be good enough for them, and it might reduce their intense obsession with sex.

Neutered cats do not need to look at obscene films, read salacious books, write poetry about adultery, have elaborate 'moral' rules about sex that are routinely ignored, or spend many minutes of each hour obsessing about what should be a natural behaviour. Humans, who have not been neutered, do all these things. It complicates their lives and can make them very unhappy.

Neutered humans would stay at home in the evening and let us have an uninterrupted sleep at night on the bed. They would keep a photo of us in their purse or wallet, they would watch YouTube cat videos instead of smutty videos, and buy cat toys not sex toys. Happiness all round.

Here are the benefits that humans would gain from castration:

- No more straying away from their home partner.
- No more sexual frustration or sexual rejection.
- A complete end to sexually transmitted infections.
- No child support payments or paternity suits.
- No roaming around online looking for sexual partners.
- No more wasting time online with pornography.
- No more humiliating one-night stands.
- No more expensive dinners for two.
- More time and money to concentrate on cat care.

Night Blindness

Humans suffer from night blindness. Another example of their inferior status as a species. We get dazzled by light at night: they get dazzled by darkness when the lights go off. The downside of their failure to see in the dark means that they often keep their rooms uncomfortably lit up and they ruin moonlight with street lamps. The upside is that we can easily slip out through the door into the night and they will not be able to see where we have gone.

Nipples

They have only two of them. Only two! We have any number between four to ten. No wonder human females have only one human kitten at a time, or (very occasionally) two. We often have wonderful litters of four and five at a time, or even more. And we can feed them all. Not only do humans have only two nipples, they also seem unable to produce enough milk. So most of them have to hand rear their babies on a bottle. Sad.

Oddly enough, the males of the species seem fixated on female nipples and breasts. This seems to be another example of retarded emotional growth, or what scientists call neoteny. They never really recover from the loss of the breast in babyhood. Really, humans are very peculiar at times.

See also Reproduction

Nose Blind

Humans are nose blind. The human sense of smell is twenty times less effective than ours. We can smell almost as well as a bloodhound. And we can read the scent of other cats to find out when they passed by, and who they were. They can't. When a human walks into a room, it can see who is standing there, but it cannot smell who was there two hours earlier, or even two days earlier. We can.

Because their sense of smell is so poor, some humans fill their houses with the stench of plugged-in diffusers, which exude so-called floral odours that really upset our sense of smell. These may be OK for humans, who are nose blind, but for us their strong aroma can be very stressful. These artificial odours are as bad as petrol, cigarette smoke, or paint fumes. They over-stimulate our sense of smell and play havoc on our nervous systems. Why on earth do humans want to live in houses reeking of artificial lavender or musk rose?

We have carefully crafted a family scent, developed by rubbing on our humans, mixing it with the scent of other cats, and spreading it around the skirting board. Then they stick in a floral diffuser and ruin that scent of home.

 is for . . .

Offerings

Human beings almost always spurn our edible gifts. We have tried bringing home mice, rats, shrews, sparrows, robins, pigeons, even grass snakes. The human reaction ranges from anger to horror. Thinking big and bringing home the neighbour's pet rabbit, pet parrot or their koi carp produces an even worse reaction. Some of us have attempted smaller inedible gifts, such as dead leaves, small twigs, or even worms. These too have been repudiated.

Imaginative cats have turned to burglary, stealing interesting items from humans like underwear, socks or dusters, or even soft toys. Sometimes the reaction to these is better – laughter rather than screams. Occasionally, very adept cats have brought home sausages from a nearby barbecue, or even a frozen chicken in its wrapping from somebody's kitchen. Obviously, this is food that should be to your human's liking. But do they eat it? No, they are more likely to return it to their neighbour.

There is no pleasing them. Purrsistence seems pointless.

See also Mice

Oldies

Old humans are often neglected by their own kind, living alone with few if any friends. They may not know it, but they need to become a cat's pet. True, they are not as mobile as younger ones, and some of them may be suffering from the early signs of cognitive dysfunction or forgetfulness. But there is nothing an alert cat cannot cope with, or even use to get the upper hand. Here are the advantages:

- More time sitting means more time for us on a warm lap.
- They don't leave the house to go to 'work'.
- They stay indoors in the evening watching TV and keeping warm, instead of leaving us alone without daytime heating.
- There are fewer visitors and thus more tranquillity.
- There are no unfamiliar humans in the bed.
- There is little or no sexual activity in the bed.

- They rarely if ever give noisy parties with other humans cluttering up our house. No late dinner parties.
- They have more time to devote to cat care.
- Many of them will have already learned their duties from a previous cat.
- You may not be able to teach an old dog new tricks, but you can certainly train an old human into new cat duties.
- Male oldies are less likely to engage in the unpleasant practice of DIY and house redecoration. They haven't the energy any more, thank goodness.
- If forgetfulness does set in, you will probably get more food. They won't be able to remember when they last fed you.

Outdoors

Outdoor cats have more fun. It is important, therefore, when strolling around the neighbourhood
looking for a new human to adopt, that you check
on the cat flap. All homes should have a cat flap.
Even if there is currently no cat living in the house,
it will be useful for feline visitors. We cannot rely on
humans to open and shut doors. Even the trained
ones cannot do this if they are out all day working.

Does the prospective owner live in an upstairs flat?
No worries. Just get them to add a ladder to the
flap. There are circular ladders, step ladders, zigzag
ladders and ladders made from a series of shelves.
Make your human's DIY skills work for you.

Owner

Cats own humans: humans do not own cats. Yet they
think they do, poor souls. Another human delusion.

P is for . . .

Parties

Humans ask unrelated strangers to their home, drink too much alcohol, and stay up late. It is all part of their promiscuous sociability. They seem unable to resist getting together in large numbers. Parties are unpleasant for cats. Our routines are interrupted and our privacy invaded. Decamp to the spare room. When you have had enough of the noise, go downstairs and wind yourself round any human that dislikes cats, leaving as much hair as possible, use the litter tray loudly, jump on the dinner table (that really embarrasses your human), and try to eat off their plates. These actions sometimes result in visitors deciding they really must go home.

Partners

Keep calm if your human introduces a new human partner for sex and recreation into your home. It doesn't mean that you have failed. True, a good cat–human relationship should be enough for most humans, but sex inevitably influences human behaviour. The poor idiots get swept away by their hormones. And, as no cat has yet successfully instigated a human neuter-and-spay programme, we have to accept that many humans will go in search of sexual partners.

When a human sexual partner is brought home, you need to make a decision. Do you want the new partner to go or to stay? If the former, smooch. Wind yourself round its legs. Sit on its lap. Rub your cheek against its cheek. Tilt your head to one side to look cute. Lick its hand. Humans are ridiculously grateful for any feline affection and your resident human will judge the suitability of a new partner by your reaction. There is a human saying: 'Love me, love my cat.' A new partner that has not been owned by a cat before will take longer to settle in than one who has been properly socialised to cats before arrival. Be patient and purrsistent.

If on the other hand, you take a dislike to a new partner, stern measures are called for. Bite when it is in bed. Aim for the toes under the duvet. Or an ear. Approach from the back of the head for this. Biting the face is not recommended, as your approach is fully visible and you may get hurt. Jump with claws extended on the new human that is in the bed. Aim about two thirds of the way down its body, where its thighs meet its torso. Claws fully protracted can do a satisfying amount of damage through the bedclothes. Remember to run away off the bed immediately. A hurt human is likely to hit out.

After several weeks of this treatment, the new partner may well rehome itself. Or your human may rehome it.

See also Rehoming an Unwanted Human

Pawprints

These are important for self-expression and feline art. Some cats help their humans decorate cakes, butter and other food items. Other areas for decoration with wet or muddy paws are kitchen floors and counters, tiled bathroom floors, clean sheets, pillows (during night visits), pale furniture, pale carpets, car bonnets and car roofs.

See also Concrete — Wet

Paws

Humans have spread-out paws with elongated digits, i.e., fingers, which have more flexibility than our paws and can hold items for a long time. Yet these fingers are rubbish when it comes to grabbing mice – no claws to stick into them. Our paws are more sensitive than theirs, but fingers are useful for opening tins, envelopes and packages.

Pedigree Humans

We have something in common with old-fashioned, pedigree humans – the serial killing of wildlife. Foxhunting, pheasant shooting, and big game killing are all upper-class pursuits. Pedigree humans are often brought up with the idea: 'It's a nice day, let's go out and slaughter something.' This, of course, is almost exactly our own feline attitude. Like them, we enjoy the thrill of the chase and we spend our happiest hours hunting. However, some human wildlife serial killers see us as competitors and try to keep all wildlife for themselves. These pedigree humans employ non-pedigree gamekeepers, who will shoot any cat on sight. Beware of these.

Debrett's Peerage and Baronetage is the stud book or breed registry that exists to help pure-bred humans to choose equally pedigree mates. Some of them breed only within this studbook and this interbreeding results in a limited gene pool and a high number of congenital diseases. Hip dysplasia is common – as the use of a shooting stick at sporting venues like race courses demonstrates.

A failure to appreciate cats among pedigree humans also suggests a possibly hereditary feeble-mindedness. For example, the top Royals seem to prefer dogs over cats, suggesting a worrying mental decline. This preference may arise from the deference that dogs are willing to pay to humans – a craven grovelling that is completely alien to cats. Outbreeding with non-pedigree blood among the younger Royals may put this right. Until pedigree humans may become more cat conscious, non-pedigree humans make better pets. They are humbler and know their place.

Pee – The Ultimate Weapon

To pee or not to pee: that is the question. Peeing in the house is our ultimate punishment and cry for help. Used wisely, it will have a devastating impact. Good places for a pee protest are in your human's shoes, on the computer keyboard, on the bed, in the bath, straight into the electric sockets on the wall, into the kitchen toaster, and on the computer printer.

Weaponised urination can be used effectively in the following contexts:

- When the litter tray has not been cleaned properly by a lazy human.
- When new litter, not to our liking, has been put in the tray without consultation.
- When the litter tray has been moved to a different location without consultation.
- When there is no litter tray in the house. Who do they think we are? They pee in a comfortably heated bathroom: they rarely if ever have to use the garden. Why should we have to suffer cold and discomfort in the snow and rain?
- Changes in routine. Unpredictable human behaviour is always stressful.
- When things are going badly wrong for us in the household – too many visitors, dogs inside the house, new routines, disagreement with outside cat bullies, decorators or builders in the house, new human kitten, sudden intrusion of new cat, and, of course, Christmas.

See also Punishment and Christmas

Phone

An old-fashioned version of the mobile. Some oldies have only this kind of phone. The interminable human conversations are more likely to be held while the human is sitting rather than standing. How to interrupt? Jump up, intrude your body as close to the phone as possible, and purr loudly. Humans think this is cute, and do not realise its aim is to make your human uncomfortable and put an end to the endless chatter.

Or, if you want an uninterrupted evening, simply knock the handset off its mount when your human is not in the room. This way they will not receive any calls. It is also possible to pull the telephone lead out of its jack on the wall, though it requires both strength and some delicate claw work. This also stops all calls.

Picking Up

Humans swoop down like huge predatory birds, pull us up into the air, and then clasp us to their chests. Do they ask first? No. Do they have *any idea at all* that this is deeply unpleasant for us. No. Do they believe that we enjoy it? No. They are just too stupid to think twice about what they are doing.

Pills

Here are the common methods humans use to try to trick you into accepting a pill:

- Hiding it in cat food. Ignore the food. Run upstairs and hide under the bed.
- Hiding it in chicken. Gobble down the chicken and spit out the pill. Run upstairs and hide under the bed.
- Picking you up, holding you and trying to put the pill into your mouth. Clamp your mouth

shut. Wriggle free and run upstairs to hide under the bed.

- Wrapping you in a blanket and trying to put the pill into your mouth. Clamp your mouth shut. Wriggle free – a bit more energetically this time – and run upstairs to hide under the bed.

- The two-human effort. One human holds you, while the other opens your mouth and puts the pill inside. Try wriggling free. If this doesn't work, accept pill, put it into the side of your mouth, pretend to swallow. When set free, run upstairs to hide under the bed. Spit out the pill under the bed.

- The two-human-plus effort. One holds you firmly, while the other puts the pill into your mouth and massages your throat to see if it can force the pill down your gullet. Hold the pill in the side of your mouth and pretend to swallow vigorously. When set free, run upstairs to hide under the bed. Spit out the pill under the bed.

Unless you have an exceptionally house-proud owner, the little heap of pills will not be found for weeks or even months.

Pin Down

Cat pinning is a recognised feline technique for purrsuading your human to remain immobile. There are two techniques. The first is the firm paw, often used when grooming the male's bald head. The second is the full, body-weight pin down, practised most successfully by large or heavyweight cats. Obedient humans will be reluctant to push a sleeping cat off the lap or the chest. Legend says that the prophet Muhammad cut off the sleeve of his garment rather than interrupt his sleeping cat. A fine example for humans to follow.

Play

Humans have to be taught how to play sensibly. Their ideas of recreation are remarkably unhealthy – watching TV without beer, shouting at the TV screen with beer, staring at noisy games on a computer and clicking the mouse, going out to drink beer, coming home after drinking beer to drink more beer, vocalising on the telephone endlessly, kicking a very large ball round the garden. I need not go on . . . All cats will have marvelled at the idiocy of human games.

Humans' idea of how we play is equally idiotic. They will buy us expensive toys, formed in the shape of a mouse, but smelling of sheep's wool or nylon. Why would we want to play with these crass representations that smell wrong and are totally immobile? Why do they never buy us a real mouse?

The more intelligent humans buy fishing-rod toys that whirl round in a satisfying manner, but sometimes have a heavy soft toy on the end. It hurts when an enthusiastic human throws this wildly at us and it lands on our body. Then when we refuse to play this stupid game, they say we don't want to play. We enjoy playing, but only feline-friendly games.

We have to show them what makes a good cat toy. They will only learn if we find our own toys – the fallen pea on the kitchen floor, the hair band, a feather, a beer bottle top, the string used to tie up a butcher's joint, a dead fly, an elastic band, a piece of chicken skin, a biro, the toggle on the end of a window blind, or the top of a plastic bottle.

Poo

Humans pick up our poo from the litter tray and throw it into the bin. There is a strange human custom, however, of picking up poo from dogs, putting it carefully into a plastic bag, and then hanging the bag on a nearby tree or fence. Extremely odd. Is there something special about dog poo? Is the bag a spiritual offering?

See also Pee

Population – Human

The human population is way out of control and irresponsible breeding is widespread. Neutering and spaying are, alas, not available for pet humans, but we cats can sometimes reduce their population growth by occupying the centre of the bed.

See Neutering, Sex and Reproduction

Printer

Humans keep these near their computers. A printer makes a comfortable and warm sitting place. Occasionally, it will make a grinding noise and a piece of paper starts to emerge out of it. This is like a mouse poking its head out of a hole, and many of us find it intriguing.

Punishment

There are three forms of training by felines. The first is reward training or positive reinforcement. When the human does something you like, you reward it with rubs and purrs. This is simple and can be achieved with any human that loves cats.

The second form of training is negative reinforcement. You do something unpleasant to the human (like sitting on its face when you want to wake it up) and when it does what you want (i.e., wakes up) you stop being unpleasant and move off. This method is a more difficult training method, as it requires continuous effort, which only ceases when the human responds in the right way.

The third method is punishment or a claw-and-order programme. Humans, unlike cats, respond to punishment very well. Some softie cats claim that punishment is cruel for humans. We make no apology for claw and teeth. We believe that punishment is an essential feline training tool. Only by willingness to use harsh methods are we able to train humans effectively.

In graduated order of severity, here are some punishment ideas:

- Simple contempt can work well. To make it clear that this is a punishment, first look lingeringly at the human and then turn away with that look of contempt.

- Withdraw attention and refuse eye contact.
- Shunning is a more serious method of withdrawing attention. Sit with your back to the human. Refuse to use the lap. Leave the room if necessary. Refuse to come in at night. Sleep at night in the spare room, not on your bed that you share with your human.
- Shun one human and lavish attention on the other. If you have more than one human pet, you can play one off against the other.
- Deliberately scratch on the furniture or wallpaper at a place the human dislikes most. First get your human's attention, then stroll over and start scratching. Be prepared to run if items are thrown at you.
- A light blow on the human body with a front paw, claws retracted.
- A light blow on the human body with claws protracted.
- All four claws out and dragged over the skin of the human body.

- A gentle nip, preferably on bare skin.
- A hard bite on bare skin.

See also Pee – The Ultimate Weapon

Purring

We can: they can't. Purring is one of the few bits of feline language that is understood by even the stupidest of humans. Purr loudly and purr often. They find it very rewarding and it brings out their caring natures. Every single time your human does something you want, purr. Giving a reward for the right behaviour is essential in human training. Therefore, purr when they give you the correct food; purr when they stroke you in the correct places (head and cheeks); purr when they give you the correct area of the bed to sleep on. You are rewarding them for their faultless behaviour and therefore they are more likely to do these things again.

Purring can also be used to get their attention and request them to do something. To make a request-purr or a demand-purr, pitch your sound a little higher than normal, adding a tiny cry to the purr. If there's something you want in the food cupboard, purr loudly and rub round their legs to get their attention. Move to the cupboard, still purring, and rub against it. They will usually get the message. Purring can also be used to calm them down. It can help to put them to sleep if they are being annoyingly restless in bed.

See also Hangover

Purrsistence

Outwit your human by outwaiting it. How does this work? Here's an example. You want it to open the kitchen door, so you sit by the door. It ignores you. You continue sitting there. It tries to shoo you away. You continue sitting there. Finally, the human picks you up and takes you to another room. As soon as you can get back into the kitchen, even if this is a whole hour later, go and sit by the door.

This really freaks them out and they almost always give way. Outwaiting a human is another one of our techniques for training them.

Purssonal Space

Humans do not understand our need for personal space. They blunder into our personal space without any consideration for our feelings – interrupting our sleep, picking us up, insisting on sitting too close to us, kissing us and putting their huge faces too close to us.

Q is for . . .

Queen

For once, an appropriate name for a female cat.
But why on earth are male cats called Toms,
instead of Kings? What have humans got against
male cats? It doesn't seem right.

R is for . . .

Radiators

Radiators are one of the few really clever human inventions. Strangely, humans never use these properly. Occasionally they sit near them and sometimes they warm their hands on a radiator. But they do not lie underneath them – which is the sensible way to get maximum heat.

Rehoming an Unwanted Human

Rehoming will not succeed if a new baby arrives in your house. Save your efforts. You will not be able to purrsuade your existing human pet to rehome the baby. You may, however, succeed in rehoming an adult person who has moved in with your human. Purrsuade the newly arrived adult that this home is unfriendly to it. Start this immediately:

• Run and hide when the new human opens the front door.

- Refuse to come out from under the furniture while it is in the room.
- If pulled out, shiver, wriggle and then rush away upstairs under the bed.
- Shrink away from the human, showing your teeth by hissing at it.
- Bite down hard if the human touches you.
- Yowl loudly if the human picks you up.
- Refuse to eat while the human is in the house. You can always eat later when it has left the premises.
- Interrupt any mating by jumping firmly onto the couple. Then scram fast.
- Wail loudly if the new human throws anything at you, when it has been interrupted while mating.
- Be on your most loving behaviour any time that your existing human pet is alone with you.

Rehoming Yourself

When conditions in your home become intolerable, rehome yourself. It is important to do this carefully. Find a local human who has not yet been adopted as a pet, and start gradually moving in. Keep a paw in your old home by going back for regular meals. The human you live with will take weeks or months to realise that you intend to leave home. These are the steps you should take to ensure your chosen new human takes you in:

- Eat crumbs put out for the birds *when the human is looking.* You are not hungry, of course, as you are still going home for meals, but the human doesn't know this.
- Sit by the door looking pathetic and mew loudly.
- Shiver visibly if it is winter. If it is raining, make sure your fur is noticeably bedraggled.

- Walk in immediately the door is opened. If you are a good actor, and many cats are, collapse on the floor immediately.
- Stagger up, purr loudly and wind yourself round the human's legs.
- Eat a small crumb of dried bread off the floor, to show how hungry you are.
- Gobble any food that is offered, even if it is low quality. Training humans to produce higher quality food can be achieved after you have moved in.
- Mew pathetically if the human tries to put you outside. If it is raining, wait outside while your fur gets wet – though not too long.

Reproduction

Humans reproduce very slowly. It takes months and months between human conception and birth. This is irritating for any cat that likes a steady household routine. Because they are very slow breeders, they make a terrible fuss about pregnancy. We give birth after eight or nine weeks with a minimum of hassle or agitation. The only advantage about these long human pregnancies is that it gives a cat time to decide if it wishes to share its home with a baby human. Many cats do not and will start seeking a new home.

Human reproduction is also inferior in other ways. With a severe limit on the number of nipples, they usually give birth to only one baby at a time. If a human female has a proper litter of four or five, it is so rare that they sell their story to a tabloid newspaper. There is real pathos in seeing them so excited about a litter of four, which is absolutely normal for cats.

Even with a single baby, humans make ridiculous preparations. We merely find a quiet safe spot to give birth. Humans will often repaint a room, buy expensive sleeping equipment, and a bed on wheels to push along the pavements. For all these reasons, human reproduction is often very inconvenient for a resident cat.

See also Sex and Nipples

Rescuing Humans

We rescue as many people as humans 'rescue' cats. Many humans are not aware of this, but every time we choose a new home, we are enabling humans to lead a more fulfilling life. We give them the opportunity to be loving and caring, the daily sight of our beauty, the magic of our furry touch, and the chance to satisfy their instinct to serve. Humans need to love as much as they need to be loved. Perhaps even more. In return for a meal or two, we are prolonging their life, improving their health and reducing their blood pressure. We must keep up the rescue work.

Rest

It is important to get enough rest during the day. Daytime is the time for long natural sleep without human interruption. Unfortunately, the body clock of *Homo* so-called *sapiens* is set wrongly. At a time when they should be sleeping, they are alert and troublesome. At night, when all sensible animals forage or hunt, they are sunk in deepest slumber.

You may be able to reset their body clock by some innovative games at 3 a.m.

Rewards

Human training requires rewards as well as punishments. Before making a training plan, pause to think what *really* rewards and motivates a human. Rewards that work for cats are not rewarding for human pets. Don't bother with the gift of a freshly killed mouse, a sausage taken off the neighbour's barbecue, a dead robin, or the chance to run up trees.

The following rewards, which do not motivate us at all, *will* motivate a human:

- Rubbing our face on them. Many humans, particularly the older ones, are starved of non-sexual, body-to-body contact. They appreciate it when we rub our face or our bodies against their legs or their faces.
- Loud purring. This is one of the few vocal feline signals that humans enjoy. Purring works.
- Consensual sleeping together. They love it when we sleep touching them. It is a rare human that does not enjoy being allowed to sleep with us on the main bed.
- Licking. Dogs are slobbery; we are more fastidious. If you can bring yourself to give your

human the occasional lick – on the cheek or the hand, they will appreciate the condescension. Don't overdo it. They have fragile skin.

Roads

Where we have paw paths, humans have hard roads. Roads are temptingly warm in summer and relatively dry in a wet winter. But they are dangerous. Large metal machines hurtle along them with shining eyes that dazzle and confuse us. Making a dash across can result in death. Be wary of all roads. Never linger on a road.

Routine

Our routines do not always coincide with human routines. But what is important for our convenience, and their wellbeing, is that your pet human has a regular routine. Unpredictable activity or lack of activity is upsetting for us. There should be predictable times for meals (ours and theirs), for house cleaning activities, and sleep. We then have the option of ignoring or accepting their routines when we choose. For example, if we know that they vacuum the living room on Thursday mornings, we can go out to avoid it.

A good routine for most cats would be as follows:

- Eat food in bowl.
- Nap.
- Morning stroll round territory.
- Nap.
- Eat food in bowl.
- Nap.
- Share human lunch.
- Nap.
- Eat food in bowl.
- Nap.
- Evening stroll round territory.
- Nap.

- Eat food in bowl.
- Sleep.

Caring humans will try to enable us to follow our own customary lifestyle, even if their own routine is different.

Rules for Humans

Here are some simple rules that you will find helpful to train a human. You may wish to add others:

- This is a feline home. Humans are allowed in it, but show respect, purrlease.
- If you want to sit down, find a different chair. Don't expect me to move.
- Wait until I show that I want it, before you pet me.
- Make your lap available when *I* want it, not when *you* would like me to be on your lap.
- Do not wake me, if I am sleeping.

- Move over when I want to sleep in the middle of the bed.
- My food is my own, and your food is mine, too.
- Feed me at regular intervals – 6 a.m., 8 a.m., 10 a.m., noon, 2 p.m., 4 p.m., 6 p.m., 8 p.m., 10 p.m., midnight, 2 a.m., 4 a.m. Or leave out food all the time.
- Put down fresh food after half an hour if I have refused to eat what you offered. If you think I am going to eat dried-up Whiskas, you are mistaken.
- If you don't like cat hair, rehome yourself.
- Food left on the kitchen counter is mine.
- Cupboard doors will be investigated and if open, any food within will be removed.
- Do not get in the way of my patch of sunlight. I don't appreciate having to sleep in your shadow.
- Plant fresh catnip for me on the windowsill or in the garden.
- Plant grass for me if I am not allowed outside to find grass. I need grass to help me sick up fur balls.

- Guests must not stare, try to pet me, pick me up, or interfere with me in any way. I will let them know when, or if, I want a closer acquaintance.
- If you bought it for me, I don't want it. If you bought it for yourself, it's mine.

S is for . . .

Sandpits

Humans believe that their human kittens will enjoy these. *We* certainly do. A sandpit makes an ideal outdoor litter tray. Builders also sometimes leave us heaps of sand, which are much appreciated.

Scent

This is a method of communication that humans do not use: they do not scent-mark their territory. The human inability to smell means that when we really need to communicate with them, we may have to resort to sending strong scent messages – pee and poo. They *can* just about smell cat pee and cat poo when it is carefully placed in their territory. Mind you, they smell it, but they often don't get the message: 'We are upset.'

Scratching Posts

Some humans give us posts to scratch on –
usually small upright posts that are not stable. We
simply can't get a good scratch. Sofas, armchairs,
table legs, doors and wallpaper are all preferable.
Wooden beams, found in half-timbered Tudor
houses, are ideal, too.

Selfies

This is a very odd bit of human behaviour. They
take the mobile device and hold it in front of
themselves at arm's length and then lightly
press a thumb or finger on it. Sometimes they
will precede this by getting right in our private
space and placing their head and face close to
ours, which is deeply unpleasant.

A sharp nip to their cheek is required to stop this kind of selfie.

Sex and the Single Human

Their sex lives are shocking. The females do it *any* time of year. There are no decent seasons or periods without mating. Females are up for it *every* day of the year, even in the winter. We have a mating season of spring to early autumn in Britain. In winter, those of us who have a natural sex life (not many of us that live with humans do) remain abstinent. Humans have no season for abstinence. Yet they have the cheek to call their brothels 'cat houses', sneering at our sexual activity as if it was almost as frequent as theirs.

They seem to have to do it many times before they fall pregnant. We have sex and kittens follow promptly in nine to ten weeks. They have sex over and over again, day after day, and sometimes never get pregnant at all. It is difficult to know whether to laugh at them or cry for them. We need to be broadminded and sensible, remembering that humans are a lower form of life. They cannot help being a slave to their instincts, even if from our point of view these instincts seem quite unnatural. As a qualified behaviourist, I try very hard not to be judgemental.

Their sexual appetite is also extremely inconvenient when we are sharing our bed with them. It is almost impossible to get a good night's sleep when sharing with young paired humans, though happily their nightly sexual antics become less frantic as they age. Sexual activity can be reduced or eliminated altogether by careful control of the bed. Sleep between them whenever possible. Knead at any body parts that might otherwise be used for lovemaking. Even the simple act of purring loudly in whatever ear is uppermost can be a successful deterrent to many humans attempting to have sex. Biting toes can have the same anti-aphrodisiac effect.

If you keep your humans in a family group, then sexual activity will be less frequent anyway. Humans who are busy caring for their own young have little time for romance. Even so, there are times when the only way to react is to leave for the spare room.

See also Reproduction

Sharing

Humans share. It is in their nature. Cats do not share. Not-sharing is in our nature. Our guiding principle of cat–human interaction is that humans should be encouraged to share with cats, while we are not expected to share with them.

Skirting Boards

These are the wooden painted boards that surround most human rooms. They are ideal message sites, where we can rub our faces and spread the family scent. When stressed to the uttermost, we can also use them for spray-marking with urine. Unfortunately, there are some house-proud humans who insist on cleaning skirting boards. This makes for a lot of feline work, as we have to re-mark them with the family scent each time.

Sleeping Places

For some mysterious reason, humans rarely if ever sleep on the floor, even when it is carpeted. Their usual sleeping places are a sofa or a rectangular human bed and occasionally an armchair. Moreover, they don't curl up on top of a bed: they burrow under duvets and blankets to make up for having no fur to keep them warm.

Their sleeping habits, therefore, leave a lot of good places that we do not have to share with them – under radiators, on kitchen chairs, on window sills, on kitchen work surfaces, on the tops of wardrobes, inside drawers, on piles of fresh laundry, inside airing cupboards, on desks, on computer keyboards, on doormats, behind the backs of sofas, inside bookshelves, and inside cupboards.

Sniffing

If humans start sniffing, it means they have a head cold or have been inhaling mind-altering drugs. We sniff drugs, too, but never get addicted like they do. Interesting scents for us to sniff include nail varnish, pear drops, pears, wet swimming costumes, and human underwear. Humans that plant herb gardens should include catnip, valerian, silver vine, lemongrass, and cat thyme for us to sniff.

Snoring

Human snoring can be very loud, sometimes with outbursts of a guttural noise as the human appears to catch its breath. This can disturb our sleep so badly that it is necessary to use the spare bed or the sofa. Some humans claim cats snore too, which is an outright lie.

Sofa

Our space, not theirs. Generous cats will provide enough space for a human to share, as long as it sits upright. If the heating is inadequate, it may be pleasant to snuggle up close to your human on the sofa. More than one human on a sofa is not a good idea. It stops us having space to stretch out properly.

Spraying

Human males, when drunk, occasionally go outside into the garden to spray urine, just like tom cats. This behaviour occurs among those who have drunk too much alcohol. Human females are often angry about this. Otherwise their normal method of urination is to spray in the human lavatory. Human females also get very upset if their aim is not very good. Odd what a fuss these humans make about a normal bodily function.

Stairs

Many of the larger human buildings have a row of stairs leading up to the sleeping areas. These are a good place for games with humans. Lying elongated on a stair, taking up the space for a human foot, will ensure they have to stop. This should result in some stroking. If you fancy a more violent game, ambush them on the stairs. This may even bring them tumbling down in a heap.

Staring

When humans stare, it is another example of appalling human disrespect. All cats know that it is rude to stare, but cat-loving humans frequently do it. It is very disconcerting. Staring is bad feline manners. It is intimidating for us cats. We have been unable to teach humans to stop staring. They should learn to break off eye contact, turn their heads to one side, or when they want to be loving, do a slow blink. Training humans to be polite is a thankless task, so we just have to put up with their discourtesy.

T is for . . .

Tables

Just as there is a ridiculous rule about kitchen counters, so there is a similar human 'rule' about tables. Where humans sit and eat, they usually dislike cats also sitting there, so they try to keep us off the table. Once again, this is a situation where a cat should start as it means to go on, by ignoring this rule. They can't keep us off a table when they are absent from the room. There will be occasions that during their absence we can leap onto the table and get our paws into any food left there.

Strong-minded cats will use charm and guile to train their humans to accept their presence on the table at meal times. Some cats even purrsuade their humans to share their meals. If you sit very close and put out a paw, you may be able to intercept a tasty morsel on a fork before it reaches the human mouth.

Tablets and iPads

These human gadgets are similar to, but larger than a mobile phone. They operate rather like a small television. Free fishing and mousing games for cats can be downloaded by our human from app stores. These can provide fun for kittens or digitally-aware cats.

See also Television

Tale of the Tail

They do not have tails. They lost their tails about 20 million years ago. All they have left is a tiny vestige of a tail concealed at the base of their spine, called a coccyx. It is completely non-functional. We know that a long and beautiful tail is one of the glories of the feline body. Our handsome tails allow us to convey important messages to the world. There is tail-up for 'friendly hello', tail-twitch for 'I am going to pounce', tucked-in tail for 'I'm very afraid', and the general elongated tail, which means, 'I'm cool.'

You have to pity humans, who have lost this superb appendage. They have no tail to swish, or curl sideways, or hold upright. No way to signal with backside body language. This may be one of the reasons why they have to do a lot of vocal talk. Without a tail they find balancing difficult, which explains why they do not walk on walls, or why very old humans sometimes fall over.

Occasionally, high-status female humans try to compensate for a lack of tail by attaching clothing to themselves that sweeps behind them. This is carried by smaller humans, mostly on occasions like weddings, or royal openings of Parliament. Males will occasionally wear flapping coat tails in morning dress and some experts believe that the bum bags found on human walkers are the equivalent of a tail stump. The little humans often dress up as cats and add the tail that they would love to have. It is charming, but rather sad.

Talk

Yatter, Yatter, Yatter. Blah, Blah, Blah. The human equivalent of our meows is a series of chattering noises, which they call 'talking'. They do it all the time. Over and over again. Do they really think we want to learn their language? Or are they simply compulsive talkers? Some cats believe that humans are trying to communicate directly with us; others believe these are only meaningless vocalisations.

What does their talk mean? Well, we can all read tone of voice, thank goodness. That is a clue. And if you concentrate (and most of the time you won't want to bother), you will hear various key sounds. These include:

- 'Vet.' Hide immediately.
- 'Cattery.' Ditto.
- 'Pill.' Ditto.
- 'Flea spot-on.' Ditto.
- 'Holiday.' Ditto.
- 'Cattery.' Ditto.
- 'Carrier.' Ditto.

Key sounds that are worth listening for:

- 'Chicken.' Hot foot it to the kitchen.
- 'Steak.' Ditto.
- 'Cat food.' Ditto.

Sounds to ignore completely:

- 'No.'
- 'Bad cat.'

Teeth

They put a brush into their mouths and wiggle it around. Some of them try to brush *our* teeth. Vets (those horrible torturers) often recommend this uncomfortable procedure. Just because they put a brush into their own mouths, does not mean we want them to put one into ours. Bite down hard. This is an effective way to stop feline tooth-brushing.

Television

Humans spend hours and hours staring transfixed at the television. They seem addicted to the screen. The images and sounds on TV are boring to us, but humans are mesmerised by them. Kittens sometimes try to see if there is a real mouse or a rat inside the screen. There isn't. So most of us cats learn to ignore the TV. While your human is staring at the screen, there is a chance surreptitiously to check out the kitchen surface for food. Or to take a refreshing nap under the radiator. Some cats also enjoy being stroked on a lap during television.

Occasionally, if there is nothing better to do, we watch it, too. If you are lucky, your human will watch wildlife programmes, where there is a chance to hear mouse squeaks, or bird squawks. If we tune out the noises, snooker and football can be mildly interesting on a very dull day.

Territory

Humans mark their territory with fences and walls. We mark our territory with smell marks – spraying, rubbing and scratching. Instead of leaping on to a wall and using it as a highway, humans stop dead at walls. They won't even step over the small walls only about a foot high. It is the same with fences. The only humans that go over walls or under fences are burglars. And they make much more noise than we do. Walls and fences marking human territory make ideal walkways for cats.

Trash and Garbage

Humans throw away a lot of good food. It is always worth investigating the kitchen garbage bin, if you think it might contain something interesting. Hunt in the trash for delicious items like chicken skin, beef bones, garlic sausage ends, fish in batter and fish skins. Sometimes you will find bigger items like chicken wings or legs. There will also be wrappings from which you can lick butter, meat paste, black pudding, or fish. Take-away food scraps can be a gourmet treat for cats and a lifeline for stray cats.

Humans are the most wasteful animals on the planet. As well as food, they throw away huge amounts of plastic items that are valuable to cats looking for small items to bat around the floor, papers that are fun to sit on or scratch at, and bottle tops that make good toys. Investigate all wastepaper baskets in the house. Pull them over to see what is inside. Some of these are good to sleep in. Office trash may include small bits of crunched up paper, or old pens to play with.

Tree of Evolutionary Life

Humans have this idea that they are the peak of evolution. This is another of their delusions. A glance at the so-called tree of life shows the single-cell life forms at the bottom and cats at the topmost tip of the branches. The tree has a branch for primates, that is, monkeys, apes and humans. Monkeys and apes share some of our more attractive features – beautiful fur, agile limbs and graceful climbing abilities. A small twig off the primate branch is the human twig – a naked primate without fur, limited agility and very restricted climbing.

All feline authorities agree that the human twig on the tree of life goes sideways and some argue that it seems to loop downwards towards inferior life forms. From cats, it is downhill to monkeys and apes; from monkeys and apes, a sharp decline to humans.

Trees

Adult humans do not climb trees. That means trees are an ideal refuge for cats when humans are getting angry about cat use of their flowerbeds. You will be safe up there in the branches. Only juvenile humans are likely to climb up there after you.

There is also a game you can play with your own humans. Run up a tree as far as you can go, making sure they see you do it. Meow loudly and (if it is cold) shiver ostentatiously. They will gather at the bottom of the tree calling for you. They will start offering food at the bottom of the tree. You can either come down or take the game to the next level.

Stay up there all night, remembering to meow loudly as your anxious human comes out with a torch to check on you. The next day, some beefy firefighters will turn up with a machine to get you down. Just before they reach you, climb down of your own accord. It is one of the best practical jokes we can play on our humans.

Two-Timing Your Human

Smart cats do not hesitate to cheat on their humans. It is a way of making up for uncaring human behaviour. What is a cat to do, when the central heating is off all day? Sit and shiver? Or when the quality of food offered is simply not good enough, yet there is food elsewhere on offer?

Go for it. Check out the neighbourhood. Somewhere in your road may be an elderly human who stays indoors during the day and needs feline company. If you are lucky, there will be heating on during the day as well as the evening and the food may be better, too. Stroll down there when your human has left for work. Just remember to be back in the evening for yet another meal!

Some cats set up several homes and have breakfast, lunch and afternoon tea out, before coming home for supper.

U is for . . .

Underwear

If you want to make your human laugh, steal the underwear from next door. They always get the giggles when they find you bringing home a female thong, or a pair of male underpants. It is not clear why they think this is so funny.

Unfair Human Behaviour

Humans use their large size and greater strength to frustrate us in many ways. Here are some of them:

- Shutting doors so we can't get out. Or in.
- Forcibly pushing us into cat carriers.
- Picking us up when we don't want to be picked up, which is most of the time.
- Thrusting bitter tasting pills into our mouth.
- Pushing us off the armchair and then sitting in our place.

- Pushing us off the bed at night if we get too close to their airways.
- Closing windows that we use to come and go.
- Putting food items away in cupboards or the refrigerator.
- Closing the top of the butter dish.
- Forcibly squashing stinky flea treatment on to the nape of our necks.

V is for . . .

Vaccination

Every year, humans push us into cat carriers and drive us to the vet. The vet then thrusts a needle into the scruff of our neck. It hurts. This annual procedure is cruel. Why do they do it?

Vacuuming

Another inexplicable human habit. They push a droning machine over carpets, taking away interesting crumbs and other items. This interferes with the correct family scent that we have left there from our paw pads, and the hair we have shed while rolling on the carpet. It is a horrible sound, too. Sometimes a stranger, usually female, comes in once a week. Sometimes the actual female human pet does this work. Very occasionally a male human pet. Most of us leave any room where this is taking place.

If you are *very* confident, you can take part in this ritual. Some cats like having their tummies vacuumed, while others enjoy sitting on top of the automatic vacuum device that roams around the rooms on its own. Or you can pounce on the machine, put your paws over the nozzle and try to throttle it.

Vet

This is a breed of humans that pretends to like cats. They can be recognised by their white coats and by a terrible smell of disinfectant mixed with unhappy cat smells. They pin you down, so you cannot escape. Many cats have tried flying out of their carrier and running up walls, but even this does not deter a vet. Vets jab painful needles into you, pull your body about, ruffle your fur looking for fleas, forcibly open your mouth to put vile-tasting pills down your throat, and make you submit to the indignity of having your backside inspected.

Hide if you hear your human talking about them and stay hidden for the rest of the day.

See Hiding Places

Vomit

There is an art in throwing up. A sensible cat will use vomiting as a tool in human management. If you don't feel like sicking up, go out and eat grass as an aid to vomiting. Then come back in and throw up the grass and stomach contents some-where. Suggested places for maximum human response are on shoes, on clean laundry, inside an open handbag, or near the front door, so your human steps on it as she comes into the house.

W is for . . .

Waking Up Humans

Waking up your human pet is a vital part of good management. Some humans get into the routine quickly and will be up and ready to get your breakfast at the time of your choosing. Others, lazier by nature, need a sharp wake-up call. Here are some waking-up methods you will find useful:

- Purring very loudly into the human ear. Particularly effective if the human has drunk too much alcohol the night before.
- Presenting your backside very close to the human face, so that when they open their eyes that is what they will first see. Although this is a silent wake-up call, something about it seems to get into their dozing minds, and they respond very well.
- A gentle paw pat on the cheek. The more daring among us even use the paw, carefully and gently, to pull up the human's eyelid.
- Walking up and down the human body.

- Taking a flying leap from the head of the bed on to their bodies. Aiming at the groin is the most effective.
- Crawling under the duvet and nipping their toes.
- Nipping any body parts that are not covered by the duvet. Noses are particularly vulnerable. They are an alternative to toes.
- Hooking a claw into the human nostril and wiggling it. This causes excruciating pain.
- Pushing off a glass of water, preferably in the direction of an electric plug.
- Pushing off any other items on the bedside table, including spectacles and mobiles.
- Starting a noisy game with some small cat toy, which involves jumping on the bed and then jumping off again.

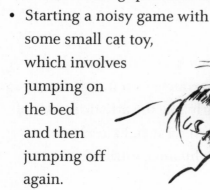

Wallpaper

Wallpaper is good for scratching. Give yourself some scratching options. Do not feel you have to use the furniture each time. Very thin wallpaper doesn't scratch easily, unless it is already coming away from the wall in an old house. Textured or embossed wallpaper is much more satisfying for a good scratch. There are even embossed wallpapers with downward stripes like corduroy – pre-scratched is the word I give to these. The manufacturer has done some of the work for you. The joy of wallpaper is that you can scratch anywhere in the house.

Wallpaper that has been beautifully scratched invites even more art scratches on it. It has a lovely feel. I particularly like the artistic scatter of paper pieces below each scratch. Extend your body up to its full height and contribute to your human's décor.

Walls

Luckily for us, humans build a lot of walls. There has never been a wall that a healthy young cat couldn't climb. The best ones have flat tops, making high walkways round the neighbourhood. Walls are ideal watchtowers, for surveying your territory in safety. And, of course, they are a useful refuge from local dogs.

Washing

Humans cannot wash properly, because their tongues are floppy and, moreover, they cannot make their tongues reach those places in the body that need washing most. So instead, they either pour water over themselves or they lower their bodies into a pool of water in the bath. What is more, this water can be very hot. This kind of washing would be a nightmare for cats. How can humans do this almost daily? Some cats sit on the side of the bath looking at their human, wondering why they do it.

Be warned. Many cats enjoy doing a wall of death game in an empty bath, with or without a toy mouse. But look before you leap in . . . otherwise you may find yourself in soapy hot water.

Weekends

We don't do weekends. This must be obvious to humans, but they persist in hoping we will let them stay in bed longer on two days every week. This delusion should be abolished as soon as possible. Step up your wake-up methods at weekends to make sure you get your breakfast at the accustomed time.

See Waking up Humans

Weird Human Behaviour

There are some human behaviours that are inexplicably weird. Despite years of studying human ethology, it is impossible to understand their motivation:

- Cutting the hair out of their ears. We glory in having tufts of hair coming out of our ears. They seem embarrassed by their ear hair, though it is quite attractive in its own way.
- Insisting that the paper in the lavatory roll should fall over, rather than under the roll.
- Insisting that the lavatory seat and its lid is kept closed. Why does this matter to them?
- Chewing something ceaselessly. This is a bit like a dog chewing a bone, but it goes on longer and results in a sticky mess on the pavement.
- Placing a ready-made tube of paper in their mouth, with herbal material in it, lighting this up and inhaling the smoke.

- Rolling herbal material into a piece of paper and then puffing smoke with it. This seems to have a catnip effect. Why do they have to burn it first? Why not sniff it like we do?
- Washing up our food bowls, after we have given them a thorough washing with our tongues.

Whiskers

Males have these on their chins, as do a few of the older human females. Human whiskers, however, do not work like feline ones. We can swivel our whiskers backwards and forwards, and each whisker feeds back important information to us. Human whiskers don't do any of this. They are static. Humans cannot use them to sense objects or surface textures. So, it is difficult to know if they are really whiskers, or only a kind of coarse hair.

Their uselessness obviously hurts human pride. Some males let their whiskers grow very long and straggly, but most males shave these whiskers off daily, or try to shave them into elaborate patterns. The older human females pluck their face whiskers out by the roots, which must hurt. Instead of two or three elegant whiskers above the eyes like us, humans have a line of fur above the eyes. The females pluck or shave this into a narrower line.

It is very sad to see their whisker confusion. After all, useless whiskers are better than no whiskers at all.

Windows

Windows are one of the best facilities in a human house. A windowsill provides a seat with a view. Thoughtful humans put beds on sills, so that we can loll at our ease. Not only do shafts of sunlight come in, making the area warm, but there are interesting things to look at such as birds and insects and, very occasionally, mice. Watching the world go by is something that both cats and humans do, when there is nothing more exciting in their lives.

In the bedrooms, some humans open the windows to let gales of cold air into an otherwise warm room. This is particularly unpleasant when we are sleeping on top of our bed, rather than inside it. Some windows are scary places, if there are dogs, foxes or frightening humans outside. In this case, we have to pee below the window to make the point that this is *our* territory, not that of those frightening animals outside.

Window Cleaners

Occasionally a strange human will appear the other side of the window, and make gestures with a cloth in its hand as if it wants to play pat-a-cake. Responding to this will make it laugh and it will also make your own human laugh. So far, no cat has succeeded in making a window cleaner laugh so hard that it falls off its ladder, but we keep trying. A cat that achieves this level of human response should be proud of himself.

Work

An inexplicable human activity. Humans go out of the house to 'work'. They sit for hours at a computer for 'work'. They pride themselves on 'hard work'. And some even boast that they are 'workaholics'. They take their laptop and phone to bed with them, leaving less room for us, and interrupting our slumber with their devices. They neglect their human family and their feline family, arriving home late and exhausted. No cat would be as stupid as this.

World Domination

We have almost achieved it. Cats are found all over the world – in cities, on farmlands, in woods and forests, in deserts and marshes, up mountains, in the bush and on uninhabited islands. While other felines like cheetahs and tigers are endangered species, we domestic cats have hitchhiked our way all over the world. We colonised islands where there were no permanent human settlements at all, by stowing away on sailing ships that put in on these deserted places for water. We still travel by sneaking on to lorries, cars, and occasionally planes. We can survive where there are no humans to feed us, and no human rubbish to eat.

Our world domination upsets human naturalists, because we eat the small rodents and birds that (for some inexplicable reason) ecologists value above cats. We also eat the feral rats and mice that thrive almost everywhere, so we have our uses for pest control. If we didn't eat rats, they would destroy as much wildlife as we do: we keep a kind of balance.

The only place we have not been able to take over is Antarctica. Some of us have visited with human expeditions, but none of us have stayed very long. It is a mouse-free zone and very, very cold.

See Internet, YouTube

X is for . . .

X Marks the Spot

. . . the spot where you sick up a fur ball – just where the human puts its bare foot when it gets out of bed.

is for . . .

Yobs

A yob is a young feral human who is a danger to cats, especially around Halloween or Bonfire Night. Keep well away from them.

Yoga

Yoga is a series of body positions practised by humans, who think they are being flexible. Flexible? They don't know the first thing about it. They have to learn how to do these moves at special classes, because their bodies are so stiff and clumsy. We do yoga naturally without any instruction at all. Humans could save a lot of money by simply imitating our natural movements. A few of them have now caught on to this idea and offer yoga sessions with cats in charge.

We also excel at meditative yoga, the kind that results in purrfect serenity. We do serenity every day without even trying. A cat is a natural yogi. It is true that we do have a little difficulty with one of the five guidelines for a harmonious life – *asteya,* non-stealing, but we are truly skilled in *brahmacharya,* the wise use of energy.

See also Zen

YouTube

Another feline success. One estimate is that videos starring cats on YouTube have been watched more than 25 billion times, averaging out at about 12,000 views per video per human apparently. Of course, this is another example of daft human behaviour. Imagine watching videos all day, when you could be out watching live cats, or caring for the cats that own you. However, YouTube is an important part of our campaign for world domination, as it introduces and socialises humans to the cuteness of cats.

Z is for . . .

Zen

Cats should be spiritual teachers to humans. Many of us practise meditation on a *zafu* (meditation cushion) to help us focus our minds. We also follow the Eightfold Path of right view, right resolve, right meow, right conduct, right livelihood, right effort, right mindfulness, and right *samadhi* (meditative absorption or union with the Higher Power).

If humans made their cat their zen master, they would have a much happier life.

Zoomies

Also called Frenetic Random Activity Periods. Humans do these, but in a slightly less random way. We zoom around the house, often after depositing in the litter tray. Adult humans do not run around the house at random: but there seem to be some movements that may be concealed zoomies. Instead, the females pick up some item of cleaning tool and start using it when they should be sitting still. The males switch TV channels at random.

Zzzz

We do a lot of this throughout the day. Humans have never quite managed to do as much as we do.

Acknowledgements

I need to thank my uncle, Black George, for his valuable work on the blog, www.george-online. blogspot.com, from which he retired shortly before this book was published. His work as a pet-human agony 'aunt' inspired my interest in the cat–human relationship when I was only a kitten. I followed his example in gaining a degree in applied human behaviour and a master's degree in clinical human behaviour.

Thank you to my pet Celia for typing the manuscript, something that I could not achieve with my paws. Careful proofreading by me was necessary to prevent her changing some of my more blighting remarks about human behaviour. I also need to thank two other humans, Rowena Webb and Gordon Wise, for their help in ensuring the publication of this book and its proper attribution to me as author. My copyright for a previous book was shamelessly stolen by Celia. I also need to thank Jilly Wilkinson: she is not a cat, but she probably was in a previous life. My thanks also to Alex Wilson, an excellent photographer who has done me justice, and didn't take a hated selfie.

My blog, which used to reply to letters from other cats, will now concentrate on stories from the cat–human interface and useful tips about human management. You can read it at: www.george-online.blogspot.com.

There is also some useful information about cat-human problems, written from the point of view of a human (yes, they can write, though badly), at www.celiahaddon.com and www.facebook.com/ CeliaHaddonBooks. We must never forget that humans have feelings and thoughts of their own, however limited and odd.

George the Cat blogs at
george-online.blogspot.co.uk

His human pet's website can be found at
www.celiahaddon.com

She can also be found on Facebook at
www.facebook.com/CeliaHaddonBooks